Contents

Acknowledgements

The author would like to thank Christine Hobart and Jill Frankel for their comments, support and encouragement during the preparation of this book, Jennie Lindon for her help and advice during the development of the manuscript, and Teresa O'Dea for reading and commenting on work in progress. The following people have kindly given permission for their photographs to be used: Marianna and Elenor Richards, Deborah and Kiron Mukherji, Dominie Constable, Ceri Lahr, Emma Thompson, Sarah, James and Peter Hodgson-Jones, Alice Moslin, Courtney and Karl Pitkin and Lucy Stow.

This book is dedicated to the memory of Eileen Newton and Anil and Tarun Mukherji.

Understanding Children's Challenging Behaviour

Penny Mukherji

Consultant editors:
Christine Hobart and Jill Frankel

Published in 2001 by:
Nelson Thornes Ltd
Delta Place
27 Bath Road
CHELTENHAM
GL53 7TH
United Kingdom

02 03 04 05 06 / 10 9 8 7 6 5 4 3 2

A catalogue record for this book is available from the British Library

ISBN 0 7487 3971 8

Illustrations by Jane Bottomley
Page make-up by Northern Phototypesetting Co. Ltd

Printed in Great Britain by Scotprint

Introduction

As children grow and develop, they gradually learn how to interact with others and how to modify their behaviour to fit in with the expectations of those around them. Within nursery settings, it is one of the roles of childcare practitioners to help children in this process. This book is written to help students and childcare practitioners understand ways in which they can help children learn using positive methods to encourage the development of appropriate behaviour.

Within the book there is a description of some of the main theoretical approaches to understanding the origins of children's behaviour, and the factors that can affect it. Although some aspects of children's behaviour have a biological basis, the family and social groups to which children belong have strong influences. The role of adults and childcare practitioners in guiding children towards appropriate behaviour is crucial.

This book looks at managing children's behaviour in childcare and education settings and gives information about the role of other professionals in helping children with behavioural difficulties. The book investigates some common situations where children's behaviour becomes a concern for parents and childcare practitioners. There is also a discussion about some of the more serious conditions that can affect children's development.

This book is written for students on childcare courses who need to look at children's behaviour in more detail than general texts can provide. The text explores theoretical issues that students on higher level courses such as the ADCE, HND, Early Years and Teaching degrees will find useful. The book also contains practical suggestions that all childcare students, including those studying for NVQs, the Certificate in Child Care and Education, the Diploma in Child Care and Education and the BTEC National in Early Years, will find invaluable. Students of other disciplines such as health visiting and social work may find the text useful as an introduction to the subject area. The book will be a valuable resource for childcare practitioners and parents who are involved in the upbringing of children.

Activities suggested throughout the book are designed to stimulate thought and discussion as well as to consolidate the reader's learning. Some activities are based in the workplace, while others involve groups of students working together. Each chapter contains case studies that translate theoretical ideas into practical situations and sections that clearly explain good practice.

ABOUT THE AUTHOR

Penny Mukherji, SRN, B.Sc. (Psychology) Cert. Ed. (FE), M.Sc. (Health Psychology), is currently teaching at City and Islington College in London. She has many years' experience of teaching on Child and Social Care courses from Foundation to Higher Education level.

Theoretical perspectives

PREVIEW

This chapter includes:

- What is behaviour?
- Innate factors that affect behaviour
- Learning theories
- Cognitive theories
- The psychoanalytic approach
- Applying theory to practice.

If you ask parents and childcare practitioners what they wish for the children in their care, you would get a variety of answers. Some might wish that the children grow up to be independent and have a good job. For others, the most important thing would be that the children are able to grow up to have satisfying relationships and, maybe, raise a family of their own. Some carers might hope that the children develop into law-abiding citizens, able to make a contribution to society, whilst for others, a deep spirituality would be important. Most of us would agree that we would want children to grow into adults who are healthy, content and able to make the most of their talents and abilities.

Because we want all these things for our children, we worry if we see children behaving in inappropriate ways and we try to influence them, so that they behave in ways that will ultimately help them to become happy, well-adjusted adults. Having a good understanding of what causes children to behave in the way they do will assist us in developing ways of helping children acquire appropriate **behaviour**.

DEFINITION

behaviour   all the activities of an individual (or animal) that can be observed by another individual (or animal)

There have been many attempts to explain children's behaviour and we will be looking at some of these approaches in this chapter. Later on in the book we will use these explanations as a basis for developing strategies to influence or modify the way children behave.

WHAT IS BEHAVIOUR?

As a child, you might recall being sent off to school or to your grandparents' with these words from your mother ringing in your ears, 'Remember to behave!'

Adults often tell children to 'behave', when really what they mean is that they want children to behave well.

Remember, behave nicely for Grandma

Behaviour includes:

- physical activities such as running and climbing
- talking and using body language
- reading and writing
- playing, sharing and co-operating with others
- fighting and quarrelling
- eating and sleeping
- using objects in the world around us.

The list is endless because the term 'behaviour' includes everything that we do or say that someone else can see.

What influences the way that we behave? This is a question that has fascinated people throughout the generations because there is an assumption that if we can find out why individuals behave in a certain way, we may be able to influence, or change, their behaviour.

We try to influence or change behaviour for a variety of purposes.

THINK ABOUT IT

Why should we want to influence or change an individual's behaviour?

- Parents and childcare practitioners aim to help children learn to behave in ways that will enable them to fit into society and acquire the skills and knowledge that they need to take a full role in society as adults.
- Politicians and community leaders seek ways of changing antisocial behaviour to reduce the level of crime.
- Health promotion organisations try to change our behaviour so that we eat a healthy diet and do not harm ourselves by drinking too much or smoking.
- Clinical psychologists are sometimes involved in helping individuals change behaviour that is preventing them from functioning normally. For instance, helping people overcome **obsessive compulsive behaviour**.
- Political parties campaign to change our voting behaviour.
- Advertisers try to change our behaviour so that we buy a particular brand of soap powder or soft drink.
- In times of war, opposing sides may use **propaganda** in an attempt to alter people's attitudes and behaviour.

DEFINITIONS

obsessive compulsive behaviour behaviour seen in people who have an anxiety disorder, when individuals have an irresistible urge to repeat certain behaviours such as washing their hands

propaganda publicity intended to change people's attitudes and behaviour, often used in times of war

When you look at the above list you can see that the ability to change people's behaviour can be beneficial to both the individual and society, but, in the wrong hands, the ability to influence behaviour could have very negative consequences.

Influences on behaviour

When investigating influences on behaviour, psychologists often look at factors that affect children before birth and those that affect them after birth. Although much behaviour is learned, there are some behaviours that appear to be **innate**. The discussion about the relative importance of **heredity** (nature) and **environmental influences** on a person's behaviour and ability, such as upbringing, is called **the nature/nurture debate**.

DEFINITIONS

innate inborn

heredity the inheritance of characteristics from parents

environmental influences the influences of a person's surroundings. In psychology, the term is used to describe influences on children such as the quality of parenting, educational opportunities as well as other cultural and social factors

the nature/nurture debate the discussion about the relative importance of heredity (nature) as opposed to upbringing and environment, on an individual's behaviour

✔ **PROGRESS CHECK**

1 List six different behaviours.
2 Why is it considered important to understand what factors influence an individual's behaviour?
3 Describe what is meant by the nature/nurture debate.

INNATE FACTORS THAT AFFECT BEHAVIOUR

When a new baby is born into a family, friends and relatives often discuss who the baby takes after. We notice that the child definitely has his father's nose or that his hair is the same colour as his mother's.

Family, friends and relatives often discuss who a baby takes after

THINK ABOUT IT

Can you think of ways that are nothing to do with heredity in which children's behaviour may be similar to that of their parents?

It is not only physical characteristics that we see passed down from one generation to another. Some children appear to **inherit** personality characteristics, for example a child may have the same fiery temperament as his grandfather. Children may also show certain mannerisms and habits seen in other family members. In one family, it was noted that all of the sons held their hands in the same way as their father when they were anxious.

When we discuss how much an individual behaves like their father or mother, there is an assumption that certain behavioural characteristics are passed from one generation to another via the **genes**.

However, this is not the only explanation.

You may have thought that a child's temper is similar to his father's because the child has copied the way that the father behaves. The child sees that having a quick temper often gets the father what he wants and is, therefore desirable. Children who have the same mannerisms as their parents may be copying them because they want to be as much like their parents as possible. Something that may start off as a conscious act may, eventually, become unconscious and part of children's behaviour patterns. In this explanation, behaviour is seen to be the result of environmental influence.

In the past, there was a debate as to whether behaviour was influenced primarily by inherited factors or by environmental factors. Nowadays it is clear that behaviour is the result of an interaction between both factors. That is to say that children may be born with a tendency to behave in a particular way, but whether or not this behaviour is exhibited may depend on environmental factors such as parenting and the way their behaviour is managed in nursery and in school.

In the next section, we will look at some of the influences on children's behaviour that children are born with, namely:

- **reflex** behaviour
- instinct
- maturational factors
- physiological processes
- personality characteristics
- inherited conditions that affect behaviour.

DEFINITION

reflex an automatic, physical response which is triggered by a specific stimulus

Reflex behaviour

All full-term, newborn babies have certain behaviours that they all exhibit. For instance, if you stroke the cheek of a newborn infant, the baby will turn her mouth towards the side that is being stroked. This is called the rooting reflex and helps the baby find the nipple.

Newborn babies have almost fifty reflexes, some of which will disappear as the baby's brain matures. Other reflexes are still apparent in adults, for instance the narrowing of the pupil in the eye in bright light conditions.

When babies are born they are tested to see that they have the appropriate reflexes, as this is a sign that their brain has developed normally. Their reflexes will be tested at regular intervals as a way of assessing brain development.

Table 1.1   Some of the reflexes seen in a newborn baby

Reflex	Description
Sucking	Babies will suck anything put into their mouths and have been shown sucking their thumbs while still in their mothers' wombs.
Swallowing	Babies can swallow from before birth. They have been shown to swallow amniotic fluid while still in their mothers' wombs.
Rooting	If you stroke the cheek of a baby, she will open her mouth and turn her head towards the side that is being stroked, as if looking for something to suck.
Grasp	If you put something into a baby's hand, she will grasp it very tight. If you let a baby grasp your fingers, you will be able to lift her up.
Moro	Shown by babies if they feel unsupported, the baby will throw both of her arms outward, spreading her fingers and arching her back. The arms then come back into the middle as if clutching something. This can be demonstrated if you hold the baby well supported and suddenly 'drop' your hands, still supporting the baby. The baby will get the impression of falling.
Startle	This reflex is similar to the moro reflex, except that the baby keeps her hands closed. It is shown as a response to a loud noise.
Eye	The baby will blink her eyes in response to light, sound or touch.
Walking	If you hold a baby so that her feet just touch a surface, she will make walking movements, placing her feet alternately on the surface.
Babinsky	If you stimulate a baby's foot by stroking the sole, the baby will fan out her toes and then curl them up.

Stroking a new baby's cheek will elicit the rooting reflex

Instinct

In the 1950s, a group of **ethologists** began to study instinctive behaviour in animals. Among the behaviours that they studied was the phenomenon of **imprinting** seen in birds such as ducks. Imprinting is the attachment shown by the newly hatched duckling to its mother and is the behaviour that leads the duckling to follow the mother duck and not get lost. When ducklings are born they are programmed to develop an attachment to the first thing they see. Usually this is the mother duck. However, researchers have been able to induce ducklings to imprint onto a pair of wellington boots, so that the ducklings follow whoever is wearing the boots. Imprinting is an **instinct**, a behaviour that is innate, shown by all members of a species.

In the early part of the twentieth century, psychologists used the concept of instinct to explain much human behaviour. More recently, it has become clear that many of the behaviours previously considered to be instinctive are, in fact, learned. However one can identify instinctive behaviour in children. The reflexes described previously are examples of instinctive behaviour, as are some aspects of physical development such as crawling or walking. It is likely that imprinting is a behaviour more often seen in the young of species that are mobile from birth and run the risk of getting lost. Newborn humans cannot follow their mothers and the process by which they become attached to their parents and carers is different from the imprinting seen in ducklings. The process of attachment is described in Chapter 2.

Maturational factors

Human infants, from every type of background, and across the world, pass through similar stages of development. For instance, newborn babies have no control of the muscles of their heads and if pulled to a sitting position their heads will drop back. As they grow older, their muscles develop. Babies develop head control and later can sit unsupported. Towards the end of the first year, babies can pull themselves to stand and soon after a year will begin to walk. The vast majority of babies will progress through this sequence of changes at roughly the same time. Some babies may pass through these stages quicker than others, depending on the opportunity for practise and their genetic make up. There are similar patterns of development seen in other areas, especially in change in body size and the sequence in which children develop teeth.

The concept of **maturation** needs to be used with caution. The original research into this area was carried out mainly on children from Europe or the USA. As research has widened to include children from other countries and cultures, it has been found that stages of development, once considered to be universal, may not be so fixed as was first thought. In addition, although the acquisition of some skills may depend on maturational factors, there are cultural differences in the way that these skills are applied.

In the 1920s, Arnold Gesell introduced the concept of maturation to describe patterns of development that are genetically programmed. That is to say individuals inherit specific instructions for sequences of development which influence growth and behaviour from the moment of conception until an individual dies.

Most textbooks on childcare and education include schedules or tables of **normative development** which outline what children can do at a particular age. These help childcare practitioners make **normative assessments** of the children in their care. A normative assessment is used when one looks at what a child can do and compares this with published material on what children of a similar age can do. It is a way of identifying children who may be advanced or delayed in their development and can be used as a basis for recommending future action. Although this is a useful approach, schedules and tables of normative development need to be treated with caution.

- Most schedules have been devised by looking at European children or children living in the USA. It is becoming clear that children may develop in different ways if they are from different ethnic and cultural backgrounds because of differences in upbringing.

- Some children may miss out stages of development, for instance children who cannot see often do not crawl.

- Children may show uneven patterns of development, perhaps performing 'normally' in all areas except one.

Critical periods

Psychologists used to believe that there was a **critical period** when a child learned to develop skills such as walking and talking. For instance it was believed that if a child was not exposed to language in infancy, he would never acquire the ability to talk. Research has indicated that children can learn to develop skills, even after the critical period has passed, but that there are times in children's lives when it easier to acquire new skills. For instance, in the first three years of life, children acquire language very easily and can become fluent in two or three languages at once. In older children, learning a new language is much more difficult and an adolescent may never acquire the fluency in a new language that they may have had if they learned it as an

DEFINITION

maturation   patterns of change in development that are sequential and genetically programmed

DEFINITIONS

normative development the description and identification of what children can do at a particular age, based on observing large numbers of children

normative assessment comparing what an individual child can do with what other children of the same age can do

DEFINITION

critical period   a period of time during development when a child is especially ready to learn a new skill. After this critical period has passed, the child may never acquire the skill if they were prevented from doing so at the critical time

infant. Instead of the concept of critical periods we now talk about **sensitive periods** or optimal times in a child's development when he is particularly ready to learn a new skill.

There is evidence from both research with animals and with humans that our brains are affected by our experiences. For example, if the part of the brain that interprets information from the eye is not stimulated in the first few years of life, it will lose the ability to process visual information. This is occasionally seen in children who have a very bad squint. This is where the eyes do not work together and instead of receiving the same image from left and right eyes, the brain receives two different images. The brain copes with this by ignoring the information from the 'wandering' eye. If the condition is untreated, the cells dedicated to processing information from that eye will lose the ability to function and the individual will become blind in that eye.

Physiological processes

An individual's behaviour can be dictated by their **physiological** state. For instance an individual can live for only three minutes without oxygen, so a person will automatically try to move away from poor air conditions in an effort to get more air to breathe. Individuals need food. Hunger or thirst will influence behaviour (although it is recognised that much eating and drinking behaviour is dictated by other factors as well such as habit and culture).

In hot weather, we automatically try to cool down

Homeostasis

Our body works best when there is the correct balance of chemicals, nutrients, oxygen and water available at the correct environmental temperature. For instance, if the proportion of water in our bodies changes just a few per cent, our brains would not function. If our body temperature varies just

DEFINITION

homeostasis a mechanism designed to keep body processes in balance. If receptors in the body detect that anything is not at the correct level, for instance water level or body temperature, then there will be a physiological and behavioural response set in motion to bring things back to normal

a few degrees, we could die. **Homeostasis** is the process of keeping our bodily mechanisms in balance and much of human behaviour is directed at homeostatic control. For instance, if receptors indicate that the body is too hot, blood will be brought to the surface of the skin and we will start to sweat. Evaporation of sweat from the skin will cool the blood. At the same time, we will seek a cooler environment, take off a layer of clothing or seek out a cold drink. Homeostatic control, therefore, involves unconscious physiological responses and more conscious behaviours designed to get the body back into balance. Our behavioural responses are influenced by our physiological state and also other factors such as convention. For instance, however hot it is, we are unlikely to strip off all our clothes in the middle of a lecture.

Babies cannot meet their own needs so their behaviour is directed at attracting adult attention. From birth, parents can recognise when their baby is hungry or in pain by the difference in the quality of the baby's cry. Babies are programmed to behave in a way that will make adults meet their needs. Later, when a baby is a few weeks old, the first social smile will ensure that parents and other adults around them will continue to care for them. Unfortunately this process occasionally goes wrong and, for a variety of reasons, parents may not correctly interpret or react to their baby's needs. When this happens, the baby may be neglected and suffer adverse consequences to her all-round development. This topic is explored further in Chapter 2 where the consequences to the baby, if parents are not able to interpret the baby's needs, is discussed.

Personality characteristics

A child's personality will influence they way he behaves. Personality will determine whether a child is shy and withdrawn or outgoing and extrovert. Earlier on in the chapter we discussed how it is possible to see similar personality characteristics in parents and their children. This phenomenon has been used to suggest that at least some aspects of personality are inherited, although it is possible that a child's personality may resemble a family member because the child has learned the behaviour from the relative. One way of finding out the contribution of heredity to a child's personality is to investigate twins.

There are two main types of twin.

- Dyzygotic twins are formed when two eggs are fertilised at the same time. These twins are non-identical twins and are no more alike than brother and sister.

- Monozygotic twins are formed when one egg splits into two after fertilisation. These twins share the same genetic information and are identical.

It has frequently been found that identical twins have similar personalities. However, this is not always the case since there are numerous examples of identical twins with different personalities, often one twin being more dominant than the other. The observation that twins frequently have similar personality characteristics does not prove that personality has a genetic component since most twins are brought up in the same environment and have had very similar experiences. One way of studying the influence of the environment is to look at identical twins who were reared apart, as the result of adoption. The reasoning is that if personality has a genetic component then any similarity in identical twins reared apart must be due to inheritance, not environment, because their upbringings were different.

The Minnesota study of twins reared apart

In an ongoing study of twins who were separated at birth and reared apart, fifty pairs of identical twins were investigated. On average the twins were separated at ten weeks of age and were reunited about thirty-four years later. They were tested for a variety of personality characteristics and it was found that they were statistically significantly more like each other than non-identical twins.

Although there is an inherited component to personality it does not mean that the environment has no effect. Experienced childcare practitioners will be able to give examples where they have been able to help a shy child become less withdrawn and more sociable, or instances where, with skilled management, a highly extrovert, boisterous child has been helped to calm down sufficiently to benefit from the learning experiences provided. This topic is explored in more depth in Chapter 7.

Inherited conditions that affect behaviour

There is a large number of conditions that affect the behaviour of children that have a genetic component. Some of these are discussed in more detail later on in the book. Conditions such as autistic spectrum disorder, Tourette syndrome and dyslexia have all been found to have a genetic component. As with personality characteristics, the fact that a child's behaviour is affected by a genetic condition does not mean that we cannot help the child modify their behaviour. Whether there is a genetic component, or not, children's behaviour can be modified by the use of established behavioural techniques.

✔ PROGRESS CHECK

1 Describe five reflexes seen in a newborn baby.

2 What is an instinct?

3 Describe two instincts seen in babies.

4 What is maturation?

5 Why is a knowledge of normative development useful for childcare practitioners?

6 What do twin studies tell us about the inheritance of personality characteristics?

7 Describe how a child's physiological state can influence the child's behaviour.

LEARNING THEORIES

In the previous section, we looked at inborn influences on the behaviour of individuals. It was noted that although there are innate factors that affect behaviour, there are other influences at work as well. Most of the behaviour that children exhibit is learned and is influenced by their environment.

In 1977, Albert Bandura, wrote 'Except for elementary reflexes, people are not equipped with inborn repertoires of behaviour. They must learn them'. As we have already discussed, biology and inherited factors can influence behaviour, but Bandura considered that the most powerful influences on behaviour are the experiences that an individual has with the world around them. In this next section we will be looking at a group of theories called the learning theories.

There are two main types of learning theory:

- behaviourist theory, which includes classical conditioning and operant conditioning
- social learning theory.

Classical conditioning

The theory of learning by **classical conditioning** was put forward by Ivan Pavlov, a Russian physiologist working at the turn of the nineteenth century. Pavlov was studying the digestion of dogs, in particular the amount of salivation and production of digestive juices when the dogs were fed. He noted that as soon as dogs had food placed in front of them they started to salivate. This is a reflex response that is designed to help the dogs digest their meal.

Dogs will salivate when they see food

One day, Pavlov noticed that the dogs had started to salivate, not when the food was placed in front of them, but as soon as they saw the dog handler enter their laboratory with their meal. Only the older dogs did this. Pavlov reasoned that they had learned to associate the presence of the dog handler in the room, with being fed. This association triggered off the salivary reflex.

11

THINK ABOUT IT

Once the dog has learned to associate the ringing of a bell with food, what do you think will eventually happen if the bell is rung on several occasions and no food appears?

DEFINITION

extinction   the phenomenon seen when a response is no longer produced when the conditioned stimulus is presented

TRY THIS!

Using the principles of classical conditioning, describe why a baby might feel happy when she sees her mother.

DEFINITIONS

operant conditioning   type of learning where the behaviour that is rewarded (reinforced) is likely to be repeated

behaviourism   a theoretical approach where psychology is defined as the study of the behaviour of the individual. Psychology is a science and scientific methods are applied. Only behaviour that can be observed is studied. Behaviourists do not study thoughts, feelings and emotions since they cannot be observed and are difficult to study using scientific methods

In a series of experiments, Pavlov showed that if he rang a bell at the same time that he presented the food on several occasions, then the dogs would salivate when they heard the bell on its own, even if the food was not presented. He said that the dogs had become conditioned to respond to the bell.

- *Before the experiment:* dog sees food (the unconditioned stimulus) $\Rightarrow$ dog salivates (the unconditioned response).
- *When the bell and food are presented together:* dog sees food (the unconditioned stimulus) *and* dog hears bell (the conditioned stimulus) $\Rightarrow$ dog salivates (the unconditioned response).
- *When the bell is rung but no food is presented:* dog hears bell (the conditioned stimulus) $\Rightarrow$ dog salivates (the conditioned response).

If the bell is rung and no food is presented, the dog will eventually stop salivating. The phenomenon of **extinction** occurs, and the conditioned response is said to have been extinguished.

Classical conditioning has only a small part to play in children's learning. Experiments have demonstrated that the baby's rooting reflex, normally triggered by a touch on the cheek, can become conditioned to hearing the mother's voice. In this instance the unconditioned stimulus (the touch on the cheek) is paired with the mother's voice (the conditioned stimulus) and the unconditioned response (the turning of the cheek and the opening of the baby's mouth) is triggered. Eventually the conditioned stimulus alone (the mother's voice) will trigger the response.

It is not just reflexes that can be conditioned. Emotions are powerful automatic responses and these can be associated with a variety of situations. For instance if a child experiences fear because a balloon bursts, just the sight of a balloon might set off a fear response, or even going into the same room where the balloon burst might have the same effect.

Operant conditioning

In classical conditioning, an existing automatic response becomes associated with a new stimulus. **Operant conditioning** describes ways in which any behaviour, not just automatic responses, can be learned. The basic principle is that any behaviour that is rewarded (**reinforced**) will tend to be repeated. For example, a baby may smile at her father. The father is thrilled and cuddles the baby and makes a fuss of her. Next time the baby sees her father she is likely to smile again because the attention she got the last time was pleasant. B.F. Skinner (1904–90) was one of the main researchers into operant conditioning. Studying **behaviourism**, he was an important member of the behaviourist movement that was very influential in the middle part of the twentieth century. Many of the behaviour management techniques used in childcare and education establishments have been based on Skinner's work but there are concerns about how appropriate it is to transfer techniques used with animals to children.

The Skinner box

B. F. Skinner experimented on a variety of animals, generally rats and pigeons. He devised a box in which animals could be tested. The box looked similar to a cage. A rat was put inside and would run around the cage, looking for a way out. At some point, quite by chance, the rat's foot would press a lever. The lever would release a food pellet. The next time the rat accidentally pressed the lever, another food pellet would be released. Very soon, the rat would learn to press the lever to obtain food. The Skinner box was altered in various ways to test animals' learning. For instance it could be arranged for the animal to receive a slight electric shock, or food pellets could be substituted by other reinforcers.

Types of reinforcement

Skinner carried out many experiments to discover the most effective reinforcers. He described **reinforcement** as being positive or negative.

<table>
<tr><td>

DEFINITION

reinforcement anything that increases the likelihood that a behaviour will be repeated. This can be something pleasant such as a reward, or the removal of something unpleasant.

</td></tr>
</table>

- Positive reinforcement is something that increases the likelihood of a behaviour being repeated because the individual finds it pleasant. Food and drink are examples of primary reinforcers, needed for the individual's survival. Secondary reinforces are things that the individual has learned are desirable, such as money and tokens.

- Negative reinforcement is something that is rewarding when it is stopped. For instance, animals will learn to press a lever to stop getting electric shocks.

It is important to remember that both positive and negative reinforcement have the effect of strengthening behaviour.

Using reinforcement with children

Original research into the nature of reinforcement was carried out on animals but psychologists were interested to see if the results of animal studies could be applied to children. An American study undertaken by Hall and Jackson in 1968 looked at the effects of reinforcement on a boy in the third grade of school. The child was considered to be highly disruptive with a poor concentration span. At the beginning of the study, the child spent only 25 per cent of his time 'on task' within the school day. The child's teacher was asked to reinforce him whenever he was concentrating on his school work. Reinforcement consisted of:

- praise
- smiles
- a pat on the back.

Reinforcement was found to have a dramatic effect and the child's behaviour improved. Eventually he was 'on task' for 70 per cent of the time.

The teacher then withdrew the reinforcement and the child's behaviour deteriorated. Once the programme of reinforcement was reinstated the child's behaviour improved again to the point where he was 'on task' for over 70 per cent of the time.

There have been many studies on using reinforcement to improve children's behaviour and, according to Robert Slavin (1991), the results indicate that reinforcement works best if:

1 you decide what behaviour you want from children and reinforce it when it occurs

13

2 you tell children what behaviour you want
3 you tell the children why you praising them when they show the behaviour you want.

The Premack principle

Research by Premack (1965) confirmed the usefulness of a behavioural management technique often used in childcare and education situations (now known as the **Premack principle**). This is where children can be encouraged to do something they would rather not do by rewarding the behaviour with a more enjoyable activity. An example of this would be when a childcare practitioner tells children that if they tidy up quickly then they will be able to have an extra story at story time.

Immediacy of consequences

Experiments have shown that a small reinforcer given immediately is, generally, more effective than a larger reinforcement given later. For example a quiet word of praise given immediately you see a child behaving well can be a more effective reinforcer than a treat given at the end of the day. Giving reinforcement immediately has also been shown to be effective in improving school performance. A study conducted by Leach and Graves in 1973 showed that giving immediate feedback to children on their work resulted in the children raising the standard of their work, compared with delaying feedback until the day after. In large infant classes this is not always possible, but the principle is easier to apply when working with smaller groups of younger children.

Punishment

Punishment has the opposite effect on behaviour than reinforcement. Punishment reduces the likelihood of a behaviour being repeated. For instance, if a rat presses a lever and gets a shock, the rat is less likely to press the lever in future. Sometimes, taking away something pleasant will act as a punishment. For instance, if a child is behaving inappropriately, a punishment may be taking away a favourite toy for a few hours or fining the child some of his or her pocket money. In a study undertaken by Hall *et al*. in 1971, a punishment technique was used to reduce the amount of time children spent out of their seats, wandering around the classroom when they should have been working. Teachers carried a clip board and recorded each instance when children were out of their seats without permission. For each time it was recorded that a particular child was out of his or her seat, a five-minute after-school detention was given. There was a dramatic reduction in the number of times that children were out of their seats, but once the punishment was removed the children reverted back to their previous way of behaving.

There is some controversy as to whether punishment is as effective at modifying behaviour as reinforcement. Some research appears to indicate that the effects of punishment are only temporary and that punishment produces aggression (Bates 1987). Most learning theorists who do support the use of punishment agree that punishment should be used only as a last resort when:

● positive reinforcement methods have been tried and have failed

● punishment is part of a carefully controlled plan

● the method of punishment is consistent and never used out of frustration.

TRY THIS!

For each of the following examples decide whether positive reinforcement, negative reinforcement, or punishment is involved.

1 A baby crawls up to a hot radiator and touches it with her hand. Her mother observes her keeping clear of the radiator in future.

2 A toddler sits on a potty and passes urine. The child's key worker praises the child and gives the child a cuddle.

3 A four-year-old uses a swear word. The grandmother says he can't watch TV that afternoon.

4 A bully pulls a child's hair until the child hands over the toy that the bully wants. When the child hands over the toy the bully lets go of his hair.

5 A five-year-old boy refuses to sit quietly during story time. The teacher tells him off and gets him to sit next to her.

DEFINITION

partial reinforcement
where a behaviour is not reinforced on every occasion, but only some of the time

GOOD PRACTICE

When deciding on appropriate methods to use when modifying a child's behaviour it is important to identify what are appropriate reinforcements or punishments for that particular child.

Childcare practitioners may feel that punishment, involving the removal of a treat or privilege, is appropriate in some circumstances, but physical punishment or the use of humiliation on children in childcare and education establishments is never appropriate both on scientific and moral grounds. This topic is looked at in more detail in Chapter 4.

The last scenario in the 'Try this!' exercise is an example where it is not clear exactly what kind of reinforcement or punishment is being applied. The teacher probably intended her action as a form of punishment, designed to reduce the disruptive behaviour. In many cases the attention that the child receives is actually a form of positive reinforcement. It has been discovered that even negative attention can be rewarding for children who feel they are being ignored.

Schedules of reinforcement

When we looked at classical conditioning, we noted that dogs could be conditioned to salivate at the sound of a bell but after a while, if the bell and food were never presented together, the dog would stop salivating at the bell. In operant conditioning, researchers have experimented to see which form of reinforcement establishes the desired behaviour quickest, and which results in the longest lasting behaviour change. There are five different schedules of reinforcement.

- Continuous: every time the animal performs the desired behaviour, the behaviour is rewarded.

- Fixed ratio: the behaviour is rewarded after a fixed number of responses. For instance a rat might receive a food pellet every fourth press of the lever.

- Variable ratio: the behaviour is rewarded as above, except every so often the number of responses needed to get a reward is varied.

- Fixed interval: the behaviour will be rewarded after a fixed number of minutes. For instance a rat may receive a food pellet every five minutes as long as the rat has pressed the lever at least once in this time.

- Variable interval: this is similar to the fixed interval reinforcement, except that the time intervals vary.

All, except continuous reinforcement, are examples of **partial reinforcement**, where a response is reinforced for only part of the time. Researchers have shown that continuous reinforcement establishes a behaviour pattern quicker than the other schedules, but once established, the behaviour is more persistent with partial reinforcement.

Using reinforcement schedules with children

Although this phenomenon was originally noted in animals, it is also seen in children. For instance, if you want to establish a behaviour pattern rapidly, then every time a child behaves in an appropriate way he should be rewarded. Once the behaviour is established, if you want the behaviour to be long lasting, then you should only reinforce it every so often. Sometimes adults unwittingly strengthen children's inappropriate behaviour because they are, unconsciously, using partial reinforcement. For example, some children have learned that temper tantrums will sometimes get them what they want. If adults are consistent in their behaviour and never give children what they want if they have a temper tantrum the tantrums will soon disappear. However, if adults sometimes give in, then the behaviour will be strengthened.

THINK ABOUT IT

THINK ABOUT IT

The theories of classical conditioning and operant conditioning were derived from experiments with laboratory animals such as rats and pigeons. Only after the theories were developed were experiments undertaken to see if they could be applied to children's learning. How might this have led to a very restricted view of how children learn?

Table 1.2 Examples of reinforcement schedules in childcare and education

Continuous Every desired response is reinforced	Every time that a child shows a desired behaviour they are praised. Every correct answer gets a tick.
Fixed ratio Reinforcement after a fixed number of responses	Children are awarded a gold star for instances of particularly good behaviour. Five gold stars wins the child a treat.
Variable ratio Reinforcement after a variable number of responses	Points are awarded to the whole class for instances of good behaviour. Points are taken away if the class is too noisy or does not listen to instructions. At the end of each week, the points are added up. Every Monday, the teacher chooses a number between 20 and 40 and hides it so the children do not know what the number is. If the final total is above the number that is hidden the whole class gets a treat. The children do not know what the hidden number will be from week to week.
Fixed interval Reinforcement of the first response after a fixed amount of time has passed	Children are rewarded for good behaviour at the end of a session, day or week.
Variable interval Reinforcement of first response after a varying amount of time	Children are rewarded with a treat for consistently good behaviour, but they don't know when this will be. Sometimes it will be after a session, sometimes at the end of the day or after a varying number of days.

GOOD PRACTICE

In early years establishments, childcare practitioners should work out a common strategy for managing children's behaviour. There is a need for a consistent approach, otherwise the staff may, unwittingly, be subjecting children to a programme of partial reinforcement, which could strengthen inappropriate behaviour.

CASE STUDY

Lina had two children aged 3 years and 5 years. Every day, at about five in the afternoon, an ice cream van toured the estate where the family lived. One hot day, Lina bought the children ice lollies from the van. The next day, when the children heard the van, they asked for ice lollies again. Lina said, 'No', because she didn't want them having ice lollies everyday. The children created a tremendous fuss and both had temper tantrums. Lina gave in and gave them ice lollies. The next day, the same thing happened, again Lina gave in and bought the lollies. This happened for several more days, the children creating a fuss and Lina giving in and buying the lollies. After a week, Lina decided to be strict and not give in to the children. She was strong for the first few days and the children's tantrums did not get them what they wanted. Their constant tantrums wore her down and every so often she would give in and buy the lollies. Lina had come to dread the time when the ice cream van appeared because everyone got so stressed and bad tempered.

1 What behaviour had the children learned that would get them their ice lollies?
2 When was the first time that this behaviour was reinforced?
3 What sort of reinforcement was used?
4 Why was the behaviour established so quickly?
5 Why was Lina's behaviour unwittingly strengthening their behaviour?
6 What advice would you give Lina to help her get out of this situation?

Shaping

In operant conditioning, an animal's natural behaviour is reinforced so that the animal learns to behave in the same way again in a similar situation. Although based on natural behaviour, animals and humans can learn complicated sequences of behaviour that would never occur naturally. Using the technique called shaping, Skinner was able to teach pigeons to play 'ping-pong'. To teach an animal complex patters of behaviour, the behaviour to be learned is broken down into very small steps. For instance when teaching the pigeon to play 'ping-pong', the first step might be to reward the bird when it picks up the bat by chance. Then the bird may get the reward only if the bat is held in a particular position. Later, the bird will have to hold the bat in the correct position, standing on a particular spot in the cage. In this way, complex behaviour patterns can be learned. Most animal trainers use this system and it is also used to teach skills to children.

Skills, such as tying shoe laces can be taught by **shaping**. Rather than waiting for children to learn to tie their shoe laces before reinforcing the skill, we tend to break down the procedure into small stages and reward children for learning each stage. For example we might show them how to make the first knot and praise them for getting this right, then we would show them how to make the loops and praise them for doing this correctly. Finally, we might show them how to tie the loops together and pull them tight and praise them for completing the entire task. In the same way, we give praise for children learning to write individual letters of the alphabet rather than expecting them to learn to write the whole alphabet before giving reinforcement. Shaping is a technique which is particularly useful in teaching children with learning difficulties and can be an effective behavioural management technique if you need to make major changes to children's behaviour. For example if you have a child who shouts out in class, does not sit still when asked and lacks concentration, it is unwise to try and change all the inappropriate behaviour all at once. It is more effective to choose to modify the child's behaviour in stages.

Slavin (1991) suggests that successful shaping depends on the following steps.

1 Choose your goal and be as specific as possible.
2 Find out what the child can do at the moment.
3 Develop a series of steps that will enable the child to get from where they are now to achieving the chosen goal. These steps will be different for each child. Some children may need tasks to be broken down into smaller steps than others.
4 Give feedback and reinforcement as the child goes along. The more unfamiliar the task, the more feedback the child will need.

Social learning theory

This theory is based on the work of Albert Bandura who worked in the later part of the twentieth century. Bandura was basically a behaviourist who accepted the importance of classical conditioning and operant conditioning as ways of explaining how learning takes place. However he wasn't completely satisfied that all learning could be explained using classical or operant conditioning as explanations.

DEFINITION

shaping the learning of complex patterns of behaviour by having the behaviour broken down into small steps and each step being reinforced

---

THINK ABOUT IT

How would you use the shaping technique to teach a child to wash their hands correctly?

You may have considered that animals do not have the same abilities to think and reason that children do. Research on animals led to psychologists neglecting to look at the contribution that thought and emotion play in learning. Indeed behaviourists considered that because 'thought' was unobservable, it was not a subject that could be studied using scientific method.

Bandura recognised the limitations of a theoretical approach derived from the study of animals and he suggested three additions.

- Learning can occur just by watching others.
- Not all reinforcement has to be external to the individual. For instance a child might be rewarded by internal feelings such as satisfaction and happiness.
- The recognition that thoughts have a part to play in the learning process.

Observational learning

Children can learn a great deal by **observational learning**, that is watching others and imitating them. If children see someone being rewarded for a particular behaviour, they are likely to try out this behaviour. For instance if children see another child opening the refrigerator and helping themselves to a cold drink, they are likely to copy this behaviour for themselves. Children will model their behaviour on others. Bandura carried out a series of experiments to find out who children were most likely to model and imitate.

The Bobo doll experiments

Bandura and his team of researchers undertook a series of experiments to try and find out who children are more likely to imitate. One series of experiments involved a Bobo doll.

In one experiment, three groups of nursery-age children were given a film to watch. In the film, they saw an adult attacking an inflatable doll that was a common toy at that time. One group of children saw a film where the adult was told off afterwards for attacking the doll. Another group of children was shown the same film, but the adult was rewarded by being given a sweet after attacking the doll. The third group of children saw the same film and this time the adult was neither told off nor rewarded at the end. After the film, the children were given a chance to play with the Bobo doll and their behaviour was noted. It was found that the children who had seen the adult rewarded for his aggressive behaviour were more likely to be aggressive themselves with the doll. The children who had seen the adult being punished for being aggressive were much less likely to be aggressive themselves towards the doll. The third group of children showed levels of aggression intermediate between the other two groups.

What influences children's observational learning?

Bandura's experiments show that children copy:

- people who are rewarded for their actions
- people who have power and influence over children, especially parents
- people who are warm and friendly towards them whom they like
- people who are similar to the children, for instance the same age, sex and race.

DEFINITIONS

role model   a term used to describe a person whose behaviour is likely to be copied by another

peer group   a group of friends or associates of the same age

When children are young, although they do copy the behaviour of their siblings and friends, they are influenced most by their parents and adult family members. Childcare practitioners are also likely to be **role models** for the children they care for, especially if they are warm and kind and the children like them. As children grow older their role models are the members of their **peer group**. The adult influence becomes less important, which is one reason why it is more of a challenge to influence adolescent behaviour.

GOOD PRACTICE

Because childcare practitioners are role models for the children they care for, it is important that they behave in ways that we want children to copy. For instance children will copy the way childcare practitioners talk to other adults and children. They will copy how the childcare practitioners act at mealtimes. If children see their key worker wash her hands after going to the toilet, or cover her mouth when she sneezes, the child will probably imitate these 'good habits'.

Children will copy the behaviour of childcare practitioners

THINK ABOUT IT

In the 'Good Practice' section you were given some examples of behaviour that children might copy from childcare practitioners. What other behaviours, appropriate and inappropriate, might children imitate?

The nature of reinforcement in social learning theory

- In observational learning, the child does not have to be reinforced directly. Behaviour is likely to be copied if the child sees the person modelling the behaviour being rewarded. This is known as **vicarious reinforcement**. Vicarious reinforcement is being used when a childcare practitioner notices a child behaving inappropriately and deliberately praises a child who is behaving well. The child who is behaving inappropriately will see that good behaviour is reinforced and will imitate this behaviour. This

THINK ABOUT IT

Can you identify where your behaviour at college or in the workplace is motivated by intrinsic reinforcement rather than extrinsic reinforcement?

GOOD PRACTICE

If you see a child behaving in a way that you would like other children to copy, make sure that all the other children see you praising the child and giving her positive reinforcement. This is an example of vicarious reinforcement and makes it more likely that other children will copy the behaviour.

phenomenon was illustrated by a study by Broden (1970). In this study two boys with behaviour difficulties sat next to each other in class. The class teacher consistently praised one of the boys every time he behaved well. It was found that the behaviour of both boys improved, even though only one child had been praised.

- In operant conditioning, reinforcement was described as being primary, fulfilling basic needs for food and drink and so on or secondary where the reward is something that the individual has learned can be exchanged for a primary reinforcer such as money. In social learning theory, another type of reinforcement is introduced. This is **intrinsic reinforcement**. Intrinsic reinforcement comes from within the individual. For instance a child may feel satisfaction at learning a new skill or they may be encouraged to persist out of a sense of pride. Intrinsic reinforcement is very powerful. Ultimately, we want children to rely on intrinsic reinforcement rather than on external reinforcement because, as they grow older, children will increasingly come across situations where there is no immediate reward for behaving well.

There have been a variety of research studies undertaken on children with the aim of training them to use intrinsic reinforcement to help them moderate their behaviour for themselves. Manning (1988) trained children who were getting into trouble for screaming out answers in class rather than raising their hands. Students were taught to say to themselves, while raising their hands, 'If I scream out the answer, others will be disturbed. I will raise my hand and wait my turn. Good for me. See I can wait!'

The role of thoughts or cognitions in social learning theory

Bandura recognised that it is too simplistic to think that just by observing someone else's behaviour we can automatically copy it. If that were the case, we should all be able to play the piano or juggle just by observing someone else.
Bandura recognised that there were five processes involved.

- Attention: the learner must pay attention to the important aspects of the behaviour that is to be copied. The learner also needs to be able to distinguish what is relevant to the behaviour and what is not. For instance if we observe a juggler, he may be singing at the same time or wearing a red hat. Both these things have nothing to do with juggling and are not important.

- Memory: the learner must store what they have seen in order to reproduce it. Young children can only copy immediately after they have observed the behaviour. Older children can store the memory for longer and will be able to postpone copying the behaviour until later.

- Once stored in our memory, complex behaviours may need to be thought about fairly often to keep the memory fresh.

- Practising the behaviour: the first time that a child tries to imitate the behaviour it may not be quite right. The child will check what they have done with the memory of the observed behaviour. If it is not quite right they may try again.

- The child needs to be motivated to imitate the behaviour, either by the hope of a reward, or for more intrinsic reasons such as pride and satisfaction.

THINK ABOUT IT

If we want to learn how to juggle, what other factors may influence how well we learn the skill, in addition to observing an expert juggler?

✔ PROGRESS CHECK

1 Explain the process of classical conditioning.
2 Give an example of classical conditioning in children.
3 What is meant by the term 'extinction'?
4 What is the difference between reinforcement and punishment?
5 Give an example of using positive reinforcement to modify a child's behaviour.
6 Give an example of negative reinforcement to modify a child's behaviour.
7 Give an example of punishment to modify a child's behaviour.
8 Explain why partial reinforcement strengthens behaviour.
9 What is observational learning?
10 Who are likely to be role models for young children?

COGNITIVE THEORIES

In behaviourist theories, psychologists are not concerned with the thoughts individuals have while learning a new behaviour. Explanations are all external to the individual, looking at the relationship between a stimulus and the individual's response. In social learning theory, there is a recognition that, if we are to understand how individuals learn, we need to consider internal processes such as attention, memory and motivation. These are **cognitive** processes, since they involve thought.

Mental representations

DEFINITION

cognitive those processes involved in thinking, remembering, imagining, concentrating and being creative

DEFINITION

mental representations thoughts in an individual's mind that take the place of an object or events in the physical world. These thoughts may be simple such as a mental picture of an object, or more complex thoughts used when we are thinking about mathematical problems or philosophical issues

Cognitive theorists consider that learning depends upon the ability of individuals to think about aspects of the world and manipulate these thoughts, rather than manipulating the physical world around them. These thoughts are sometimes called **mental representations**. A child may want to get a sweet on top of a shelf. Although the child has never done this before or seen it done by anyone else, the child may get a chair, place it in the correct position, climb on it and reach the sweet. The child has been able to think about how to overcome this problem by forming mental images and working out in his mind what might be possible, without having to experiment with the real objects first.

Cognitive-developmental theories

These theories, about how children learn behaviour are based on the following ideas.

- Children will spontaneously interact with people and objects in their environment.
- Children use their developing thought processes to make sense of these experiences.

- Children change their thoughts and actions as a result of their experiences.
- Because children's brains are developing, the way they think about experiences changes as they get older.

Piaget's theory

Jean Piaget was born at the end of the nineteenth century in Switzerland and spent almost fifty years researching into children's learning. Piaget's work still influences the way we think about how children learn today.

Although primarily remembered as a cognitive theorist, Piaget was a biologist and believed that genetics plays a part in the way we live and behave. He was influenced by Darwin's theory of evolution, which describes how animals, over generations, change physically and in their behaviour as a response to changes in their environment. This process of change is called adaptation.

- Behaviourists consider that learning is a passive process, whereby changes in the environment lead to behavioural changes in the individual.

- Piaget saw learning as an active process, where children use their thought processes to actively explore, manipulate and experiment with objects and people in their environment.

- Children explore their environment using their senses and take in (assimilate) this information.

- This information is compared with concepts they already have (schemas). The new information either confirms what they already know (a state of equilibrium) or is incompatible with the ideas they already have (a state of dis-equilibrium)

- The child modifies their existing schemas (accommodation) to make sense of the new information.

- Changes in schemas result in behavioural change (adaptation).

Children explore their environment using their senses

DEFINITIONS

schemas basic ideas or thoughts about the environment

assimilation the taking in of information about objects or people in a child's environment

equilibrium the balance between assimilation and accommodation which leads to the modification of schemas

accommodation the modification of schemas to take account of new information that has been assimilated

adaptation changes in thinking and behaviour as a result of assimilation and accommodation

CASE STUDY

Ilgun is 9 months old and has just started to crawl. He crawls to a radiator, which is turned off. He uses his eyes to see what it looks like, he touches it with his hand and it is cold, he puts his mouth to it to see what it tastes like, he smells it and listens to find out if it makes a noise. These sensations are assimilated and he begins to develop a **schema** about radiators.

The next time he crawls over to the radiator it is turned on. This time it is hot and he quickly removes his hand and cries. He assimilates the information that the radiator is hot (**assimilation**). His existing schema about radiators is that they are cold. This new information produces a state of **dis-equilibrium** and Ilgun adjusts his schema to include the information that radiators can be hot or cold (**accommodation**). The next time Ilgun goes up to a radiator he does not touch it. He has adapted his behaviour (**adaptation**). He has learned that radiators can hurt you.

This is a cognitive explanation of how Ilgun learned not to touch the radiator.

1 How would a behaviourist explain his change in behaviour?
2 Using the terms 'assimilation', 'accommodation', 'equilibrium' and 'adaptation', explain how a baby learns that you can eat a piece of toast, but not a piece of wood.

Piaget also thought that children pass through fixed stages in cognitive development in a way similar to the stages children pass through when learning to walk. Children's thinking is very different from adults' because they have not developed the ability to use adult logic, but because children pass through similar stages one can predict the type of mistakes in reasoning that they are likely to make. Children aged 5 years will tell you that there is more Plasticine™ when it is rolled into a long worm, than if the same Plasticine™ is rolled into a ball in front of their eyes. Most older children are quite sure that the amount of Plasticine™ is the same, despite its shape.

Other theorists such as Jerome Bruner and Margaret Donaldson have used Piaget's theory as a basis for their work. Nowadays, we respect Piaget as a great theorist because he has had a profound influence on the way we view children's learning and the way that we educate children. More recent research has been critical of several aspects of his work, suggesting that children may be more competent in many areas than was first thought, and casting doubt onto the fixed stages of development that Piaget suggested children pass through. It is also suggested that children can be taught certain concepts, such as conservation of matter, earlier than if they had been left to discover it on their own.

Social constuctivist model

In Piaget's theory, the emphasis is on what the child does to make sense of the world around them. His theory is called a **constructivist theory** because he describes how children construct ideas and concepts about the world around them by actively exploring their environment. Other theorists have looked at social influences on children's learning in addition to looking at the

DEFINITIONS

constructivist model a way of looking at children's learning which explains how children construct ideas and concepts about the world around them

social constructivist model a way of explaining children's learning which acknowledges the role of friends, family and other aspects of society in children's learning, in addition to the activities of the child

23

scaffolding   helping a child learn by making learning tasks more manageable

zone of proximal development   the difference between what a child can learn on their own and what they can learn with the help of an adult or a more competent friend

role of the child. This is called the **social constructivist model**. In particular Jerome Bruner and Lev Vygotsky have written about how adults can facilitate children's learning.

- Jerome Bruner (1915–) suggested that adults can help children learn by 'scaffolding'. That is supplying help to make learning something new more manageable. For instance, we can help young children learn to dress themselves by giving them clothes that pull on easily, have elastic waists and Velcro™ fastenings. We can give them articles of clothing one at a time in the order needed to put them on and we can hold each article correctly so they can put it on easily.

- Lev Vygotsky (1896–1935) believed that social relationships have a key role to play in children's learning. He thought that children would learn through interacting with their environment, but that they could be helped by an adult, or a more competent friend, to go beyond what they could learn on their own. Vygotsky called the difference between what a child could learn on their own, and what they could learn with expert help, the **zone of proximal development**.

✔ PROGRESS CHECK

Are there similarities between Bruner's concept of 'scaffolding' and the behaviourist concept of 'shaping'?

1 Using Piaget's theory, explain how a small child learns which toys will float and which will sink.
2 Using the example in question 1, explain how an adult might scaffold the child's learning.
3 Explain the difference between a constructivist model and a social constructivist model.

THE PSYCHOANALYTIC APPROACH

When we use cognitive theories to explain how children learn, we recognise the importance of an individual's thoughts or cognitions. These thoughts are conscious, that is, we are aware that we are thinking. In psychoanalytic explanations it is suggested that our behaviour is also influenced by factors of which we are unaware.

Sigmund Freud (1856–1939)

Sigmund Freud was a doctor who worked for most of his life in Vienna. Originally he specialised in neurology (the study of the brain and the nervous system) but later he became interested in patients who had psychiatric problems. He believed that our behaviour is driven by two instincts:

- libido, an instinct for life which gives us energy for survival, reproduction and wellbeing
- the death instinct, a negative force which gives us energy for aggression, anger, guilt, temptation and so on.

Our personalities are influenced by the balance between our libido and death wish. Some individuals will be positive because they have a strong libido, while others will be negative because their death instinct predominates.

The structure of personality

Freud described our personalities as being composed of three parts.

- The **id**: this part of our personality is present from birth and is concerned with survival. A baby's behaviour is largely instinctive, involving reflex behaviour designed to have his needs met immediately. The id is that part of the personality involved with the meeting of primitive needs. As we grow, the id persists, although we are unaware of it. Occasionally, it is possible to see its influence when we behave irrationally, demanding to have our needs met immediately.

- The **ego**: as babies grow older they gradually learn that it is not always possible to have what they want. The id will continue to generate demands, but children learn that some demands are unrealistic. For instance toddlers begin to realise that they will not be given every toy that catches their attention in a shop. At first, the learning process is difficult and the toddler shows his frustration in temper tantrums. Another part of the personality develops, the ego, which is rational and logical which enables children to cope. The ego will help children know what demands are likely to be met and which are unrealistic. Under the influence of the ego, the child will use his memory and problem-solving skills so that they can effectively meet the demands of the id by planning and negotiating.

- The **superego**: this part of the personality helps the ego know what is a realistic demand from the id, or not. There are two parts to the superego: the conscience and the ego ideal.

  - The conscience is what tells us what actions are wrong, what we should not do. We develop our conscience by internalising the teaching from parents, teachers, religious leaders and others in authority over us.

  - The ego ideal, on the other hand, tells us what we should do and is guided by principles of morality.

The ego has to balance the demands of the unconscious id and the influences of the conscience and morality from the superego. In some individuals, it is possible to see that the id is very strong. These individuals may be selfish and demand that their needs are met instantly. In other individuals, the super ego dominates and they may take obeying the rules to abnormal extremes.

Stages of personality development

As babies grow older, they find pleasure from different parts of their bodies, first the mouth, then the anus and finally the genitals. Freud called these areas erogenous zones. If children have painful experiences, the child's personality will become 'stuck' or fixated at this level of development, giving rise to problems later on in life.

- The oral stage: this corresponds to the first two years of a baby's life, during which time we get pleasure from sucking, feeding and exploring with our mouths. Freud thought that if we do not get the right amount of stimulation our personalities might become affected. For example a child who was underfed might become aggressive, pessimistic or depressed when older. Babies who were over-stimulated might become over-optimistic, dependant and over-excitable. Smoking, drinking, over-eating and other dependencies have been linked to fixations at the oral stage of development.

- The anal stage of development coincides with children being able to control their bowel movements. It is at this stage that children are 'toilet trained'. If toilet training is either too strict or too easy-going then children may be fixated at this level of development. Freud suggested that individuals who felt forced into toilet training sometimes develop 'anal retentive' personalities. They may be over-possessive and obsessive about tidiness or punctuality. Individuals who got great pleasure from their bowel movements may develop 'anal expulsive' personalities. These individuals tend to be overgenerous, untidy people.

- The phallic stage: this stage takes children up to about 6 years of age. Freud claimed that children start to have sexual feelings. Boys' first feelings will be for their mothers and girls' for their fathers and they will become jealous of the other parent. This is the 'Oedipus complex'. Boys tend to have negative feelings about their father and begin to fear that their fathers will be so angry that they will be castrated. According to Freud, these feelings are all unconscious. To avoid the threat of castration, boys begin to try to be like their fathers. This is called identification and boys identify with their fathers by talking like them and trying to think like them. Sometimes, if a boy's father is too dominant or aggressive, the child may grow up to be an aggressive personality because he has identified too much with his father.

- The latency period: from about the age of 6 years until the age of about 11 years, there are few influences on children's personalities. Most of their energy is taken up with going to school and having same sex friendships.

- The genital stage of development coincides with puberty. In this stage, children start developing interests in sexual relationships. In very sexually repressive societies, frustrations can lead to adults finding it difficult to relate to others in a sexual way, and they may be shy and immature.

Erik Erikson (1902–94)

Erikson was profoundly influenced by Freudian theory. He, also, proposed that individuals pass through a series of stages. Erikson saw development as a lifelong search for a sense of identity in which individuals have to face a fixed series of 'crises' or problems. As individuals move from stage to stage, they come closer to gaining a sense of identity. Erikson describes eight stages in all from babyhood to old age and like Freud he thought that unresolved issues in earlier stages of development could affect an individual's ability to cope in later stages. The first four stages, concerned with childhood, are outlined here.

Erikson's stages of development in childhood

- Babyhood sees the development of trust. Unresponsive caregivers who do not meet a baby's needs adequately might induce a feeling of mistrust that lasts throughout an individual's life.

- The toddler years see the development of the sense that we can do things (autonomy). Children who are not allowed to do things for themselves, or are told that their actions are bad or inadequate might be left with feelings of self-doubt and shame.

- Infant school years see the development of confidence and initiative. Children who are not given encouragement to be active and take the initiative may grow up to find leading an active life, with a sense of purpose difficult.

- Junior school years see the development of a sense of achievement in developing skills. In this stage. children need to be determined to become skilled. If children are not encouraged or are told that they are useless, they may never try hard to develop skills because they think they will never manage.

✔ PROGRESS CHECK

1 What two instincts drive behaviour according to Freudian theory?
2 Describe the structure of personality according to Freud.
3 How did Freud describe the stages of personality development?
4 Describe how unresolved difficulties in an earlier stage of development could affect behaviour when a child is older.
5 What are the similarities between Erikson's theory and Freud's ideas?

APPLYING THEORY TO PRACTICE

In this chapter, we have looked at various influences on children's behaviour, summarised below.

- Children's behaviour is the result of a complex interaction between innate, biological influences and environmental influences.

- Innate, biological influences on children's behaviour include reflexes, maturation, physiological processes and the genetic influence on a child's personality and behaviour.

- Environmental influences include parenting, education, cultural and social factors.

- Three theoretical approaches have been described in the chapter that try to explain the origins of children's behaviour and how children learn.

  1 Behaviourist theories (classical conditioning, operant conditioning and observational learning)
  2 Cognitive theories (Piaget, Bruner and Vygotski)
  3 Psychoanalytic theories (Freud and Erikson)

The theories described in this chapter have all had an influence on the way that we care for and educate children. Some childcare and education practitioners base their practice overwhelmingly on one theoretical approach, but the majority of childcare and education establishments will have practices that are influenced by aspects of different theories.

The following table outlines the way the different theories have been used in childcare and education.

Table 1.3   The influence of different theoretical approaches on childcare and education practice

Theory	Main points of theory	Practical application
Classical conditioning	• An automatic response such as a reflex or powerful emotion can be triggered by a new stimulus after the new stimulus has been paired with the usual stimulus that triggers the response. • Extinction is said to have occurred when the new stimulus no longer triggers the response.	Not much used in childcare and education situations although it may help a practitioner understand how children can become very fearful in some situations. Classical conditioning underpins behaviour therapy, a behaviour management technique used for treating children with problem behaviour such as phobias. Chapter 5 has a fuller explanation of this.
Operant conditioning	• Behaviour that is rewarded (reinforced) is likely to be repeated. • Reinforcement can be positive (a reward) or negative (the removal of something unpleasant.) • Punishment is something that reduces the likelihood of a behaviour being repeated, either because it is unpleasant or something pleasant has been removed. • Complex behaviours can be learned by having the behaviour broken down into small steps and each step being reinforced. This is known as shaping.	Principles have been widely used in childcare and education. • The use of positive reinforcement e.g. praise, smiles and gold stars is a powerful method of changing a child's behaviour. • Punishment is not so effective as positive reinforcement but can be used as a last resort as long as it is planned and never involves physical methods or humiliation. • Shaping is used to teach skills such as tying shoe laces or learning a musical instrument. It is an approach often used with children with learning difficulties or multiple behaviour difficulties. • Operant conditioning is the basis of a technique known as behaviour modification. See Chapter 5 for a fuller explanation. With classical conditioning, operant conditioning has been criticised for trying to apply a theory based on research into animals to children, neglecting to take account of children's thoughts and emotions. Behaviour modification has been criticised for not looking at the reasons why children are behaving inappropriately.
Social learning theory	• Children learn from copying others. • Role models for children include their parents and people they look up to and care for them such as childcare practitioners. • Children will tend to repeat behaviour if they see someone else being rewarded for that behaviour. • Children can be motivated by internal reinforcements such as pride and satisfaction.	Social learning theory has many practical applications in childcare and education situations. • Childcare practitioners are powerful role models for the children they care for. This is valuable in teaching social skills, attitudes towards others, conflict resolution behaviour, personal hygiene etc. • If a child is behaving inappropriately they may be motivated to change their behaviour if they see someone being rewarded for behaving well. • Children can be taught to congratulate themselves for behaving well, rather than always relying on someone to notice that they are behaving well and praising them. • Social learning theory forms the basis of a therapy called modelling. Chapter 5 contains more details. Although based on behaviour theory, social learning theory recognises that children's behaviour is influenced by their thought processes and emotions.
Cognitive (constructivist) theories	• Children learn by actively exploring their environment. • Children use internal processes such as attention, memory, motivation and reasoning to help them make sense of the world. • Children's thinking is different from adults and develops as they grow older. • Social constuctivists emphasise the role of social influence on children's learning and the particular role of the adult in children's learning.	Cognitive theories have had a great influence on the way that children are taught, especially in nurseries and pre-schools. The theories have influenced the way we help children relate to one another. • Children need the time and the opportunity to mix with other children and adults so that they can actively experiment with different ways of relating to others, conflict resolution etc. Adults should try to let children work out how to resolve conflicts for themselves before stepping in to mediate.

Table 1.3 *continued*

		• Because children's thinking and reasoning changes over time, childcare practitioners need a good knowledge of child development so that they understand what behaviour to expect from children of particular ages, e.g. two-year-olds are egocentric and find sharing very difficult. • Adults can help children learn by 'scaffolding', making learning something new manageable by giving appropriate support in the early stages of learning. Children can be helped to go beyond what they can learn about a situation on their own with the help of an adult. For example if children have failed to resolve a conflict on their own the childcare practitioner might offer a suggestion. Cognitive theories have contributed to cognitive behaviour therapies which are discussed further in Chapter 5.
Psychoanalytic theories	• Our behaviour is influenced by unconscious factors of which we are unaware. • It is the interaction between internal instincts and environmental influences that results in the way we think, act and feel. • Children and adults pass through stages in personality development. • Unresolved conflicts in earlier stages of development can lead to emotional or behavioural problems later in life.	Psychoanalytic theory has influenced the way that childcare practitioners help children come to terms with emotional crises and stressful events in their lives. • Children are encouraged to use play and creative activities to express emotions that they may not be able to put into words such as grief following the death of a loved one. • Books, role play and stories are used to help children prepare for big events in their lives such as the birth of a sibling, a hospital visit or a move to a new house. Psychoanalytic theory is the basis of play therapy and art and drama therapy. More details can be found in Chapter 5. Psychoanalytic theory has been criticised because it is very difficult to test scientifically. It has been suggested that some of the positive effects of play therapy may be just the effect of the child having the one-to-one attention of an adult.

KEY TERMS

You need to know the meaning of the following words and phrases. Go back through the chapter to make sure you understand them:

accommodation	id	Premack principle
adaptation	imprinting	propaganda
assimilation	inherit	punishment
behaviour	innate	reflex
behaviourism	instinct	reinforcement
classical conditioning	intrinsic reinforcement	role model
cognitive	or reward	scaffolding
constructivist model	maturation	schemas
critical period	mental representations	sensitive period
ego	normative assessment	shaping
environment	normative development	social constructivist
equilibrium	observational learning	model
ethologist	obsessive, compulsive	superego
extinction	behaviour	the nature/nurture
genes	operant conditioning	debate
heredity versus	partial reinforcement	vicarious reinforcement
environment	peer group	zone of proximal
homeostasis	physiological	development

FURTHER READING

Most introductory texts on psychology will give an explanation of the various theories that explain the factors affecting children's behaviour.

These books are especially suitable for students on Level 2 and Level 3 courses.

Davenport, G. (1994) *An Introduction to Child Development,* Collins Educational

Flanagan, C. (1996) *Applying Psychology to Early Child Development*, Hodder and Stoughton

These books are suitable for students studying on Level 3 and Level 4 courses.

Atkinson, R. L., Atkinson, R. C., Smith, E., Bem, D. and Nolen-Hoeksema, S. (1996) *Hilgard's Introduction to Psychology,* Harcourt Brace

Bee, H. (1995) *The Developing Child,* Longman

Lee, V. and Das Gupta, P. (1998) *Children's Cognitive and Language Development*, Blackwell in association with The Open University
Chapter 1 is particularly useful.

Slavin, R. (1991) *Educational Psychology, Theory Into Practice,* Prentice Hall International Editions
Chapter 4 has a useful section relating learning theory to the practical situation.

The effects of the family environment on children's behaviour

PREVIEW

This chapter includes:

- Bonding and attachment
- Separation
- Special cases involving separation: bereavement
  divorce
  imprisonment
- Parenting styles
- Parental control.

Although the way children behave is influenced by many factors, one of the most powerful influences is the affect of family. One critical factor is whether or not a child has been brought up within a family or in a group care in an institution. Many children have had positive and happy experiences in group care situations, such as in the Kibbutzim in Israel or in some well run children's homes in this country. Unfortunately, both in the UK and other countries, some children have been neglected and abused in institutions, such as orphanages, that were supposed to provide them with care and shelter. Many children were permanently harmed and were never able to form satisfactory relationships with others when they were adult. Even when children are looked after within a family they can be adversely affected by poor or inconsistent parenting and other factors that will be discussed in this chapter.

BONDING AND ATTACHMENT

Babies' first social relationships are usually with their parents and close family members. For babies to form adequate social relationships as older children and adults they need to have experienced satisfactory relationships with their parents and/or carers as infants. There are several aspects to this process:

- the initial adult to baby bond immediately after birth
- the process where the adult becomes attached to the baby in the first few months of life
- the process where the child becomes attached to adults.

The first two processes, of adult to baby **attachment**, are important for a baby's survival. It is a huge task looking after a baby, involving sleepless nights, loss of freedom and great responsibility. The adult gets little reward for the inconvenience and long hours they put into caring for a newborn baby. It is thought that without the processes of adult to baby attachment, many babies would perish through neglect. The attachment process may be nature's way of ensuring that babies survive.

The initial adult to baby bond

In the 1970s, there was great interest in the initial **bonding** process between mother and baby at the time immediately after birth. In the first few hours after birth, many newborns are particularly alert. When a newborn is held in his mothers' arms he focuses on her face and makes eye contact. The newborn has a fixed focus of about 20 centimetres (8 inches) that is just the distance from between his eyes and his mothers' eyes when being cradled in her arms. This initial eye contact can be an amazing experience and parents will often report that they feel a rush of love for the child at this time. In a very short time most newborns become very sleepy and do not regain this level of alertness for a few days.

> ### DEFINITION
>
> **attachment** in child development, 'attachment' can mean the feelings a parent or carer has for a baby or the feelings a baby has towards a significant adult

> ### DEFINITION
>
> **bonding** the initial rush of affection felt by an adult, usually the mother, towards a newborn baby, in the period immediately after birth

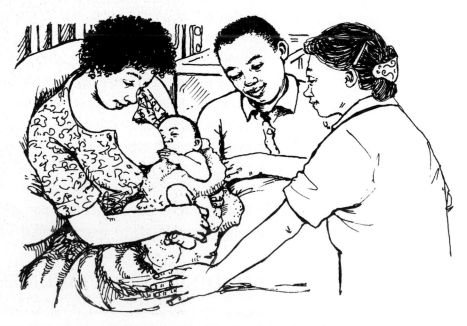

Mothers are encouraged to hold their babies as soon as they are born

Two paediatricians, Klaus and Kennell, in 1976, developed a theory, backed up with research, that if a mother was denied the opportunity to bond with her baby at this time, then there might be long-term effects on her ability to be an effective parent. They considered that this would be because her attachment to the child would be weaker.

Because of this theory, hospitals changed many of their practices. Parents were encouraged to hold the baby immediately after birth and mother and baby were not separated unless absolutely necessary. Instead of new babies being cared for in a nursery and being given to the mothers only for feeds, the babies were cared for in cots by their mothers' beds. If a baby needed special care, the mother was encouraged to spend time with the baby.

There is no doubt that parents appreciate these changes but subsequent research has not confirmed Klaus and Kennell's theory. For some mothers who are at risk of developing poor parenting skills, there appears to be a long-term benefit. Mothers from disadvantaged backgrounds, who were given the opportunity to have their babies with them from birth, were less likely to be suspected of abusing their children and their children were less likely to be hospitalised for illness or failure to thrive. For the majority of mothers, though, early contact does not seem to affect parenting skills.

Mutual attachment behaviours between adult and baby

A parent may miss out on the initial bonding process with their baby, but still go on to develop a satisfactory attachment with their child. It is crucial that the parents are given the opportunity to interact with the child in the early months so that they attach to the baby. Psychologists have discovered that babies and the adults who care for them show a characteristic behaviour pattern that Helen Bee describes as a 'dance'.

TRY THIS!

Either on your own or in a small group, discuss how poor parenting might affect a child's behaviour. Make a note of your thoughts. Later, when you have read the rest of this chapter, discuss this topic again. You may be surprised at how much you already knew about the effects of parenting on behaviour.

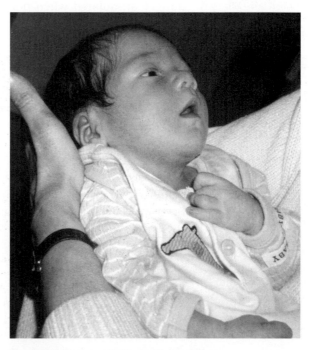

Elena at eleven days old is communicating with her father

The baby can communicate his needs by crying and the adult responds to these cries. A mother or a regular care giver soon begins to recognise what a baby's cries mean and the baby learns to respond by:

- quietening
- gazing into the adult's eyes
- smiling in response to an adult's smile, or as a way of getting attention from an adult
- snuggling into the adult
- cooing and vocalising.

The adult and the baby begin to show a pattern of behaviour where the child will attract the adult's attention, who responds with a kind of behaviour that is fairly automatic and seen only when an adult communicates with a baby. Adult behaviour can consist of:

- smiling
- raised eyebrows
- wide open eyes
- the use of a quiet, high pitched voice.

For an adult to baby attachment to be formed, the baby and adult need to have the chance for repeated interactions. Both adult and baby need to practice taking turns, smoothly responding to one another's lead. The quality of the adult/child interaction has implications for children's behaviour when they are older.

Mothers who are sensitive and responsive to their baby's needs can interpret their baby's signals appropriately. Thus the baby is fed when hungry, stimulated when bored, soothed and settled when sleepy. Mothers who are insensitive to their baby's needs or who are unresponsive or inconsistent, may care for the child more on the basis of their own moods. A small percentage of mothers may feed the baby when the mother is hungry, cuddle the baby when they feel like it rather than when the baby wants it, or stimulate the baby when the baby needs to sleep. Insensitive, unresponsive mothers tend to have babies who are unsettled and show abnormal attachment responses when they are older.

It is important that babies being cared for in childcare establishments are looked after by as few adults as possible. The **key worker system** is important because it gives the adult and baby the chance to develop a smooth pattern of interlocking attachment behaviours. The key worker needs to be sensitive and responsive to the baby's needs in the same way that the baby's mother is.

Fathers

Fathers become attached to their babies in much the same way as do mothers. Fathers show the same attachment behaviours in the way they hold and interact with new babies as mothers do and their initial attachment can be as strong. As babies grow older, the way in which fathers interact with them changes. Mothers tend to interact more quietly with babies and will

TRY THIS!

Observe a mother interacting with a baby of about 3 months old. Observe the attachment behaviours of the baby and the mother. Can you identify the way that their behaviour interlocks? If possible, use a video camera as this will give you more time to closely analyse the behaviour.

DEFINITION

key worker system   a key worker system is used in childcare and education establishments which provide group care. Babies and young children are allocated to a named key worker who carries out the majority of their care during the day and liaises with the children's parents

THINK ABOUT IT

Why do you think that fathers interact with babies in a different way than mothers?

You might have considered the following points.

- Fathers may be copying the way other fathers behave in the society around them and in the media.
- They might remember their fathers playing with them in this way.
- They might be getting approval from the babies' mothers who expect them to play differently with the babies than themselves.
- Many childcare practitioners note the difference between the way that boys and girls play in the playground. Is the difference in the way that fathers and mothers interact with babies an extension of this?

Fathers engage in more physical play with babies than mothers

talk and smile at them more than fathers do. Fathers have been shown to engage in more physical play with babies, although this does not mean that they are any less attached to their children.

Child to adult attachment

Mary Ainsworth undertook a series of studies in the 1970s and 1980s into the way babies become attached to their parents and carers and identified four distinct stages.

1 Birth to 3 or 4 months of age

Babies shows attachment behaviours but do not show that they distinguish one care giver from another. Recent research has shown that babies can distinguish between care givers earlier than this. For example newborn babies will turn their heads towards their mother's voice whereas they may not react to the voices of others. In addition, it is often noted that a baby will settle more readily with the care giver who has had most experience of caring for them.

2 Around 3 to 6 or 7 months of age

Babies begin to smile more at people who regularly take care of them and close family members such as brothers and sisters, but there are still a number of people towards whom babies show attachment behaviours.

3 Around 6 to 7 months of age

Babies direct their attachment behaviours typically to one adult, usually the mother, depending on the family and care-giving situation. The type of attachment behaviour changes from trying to attract and keep an adult's attention, to seeking out the adult. Some babies show strong attachments to both parents or to a parent and a regular care giver.

It is thought that the development of attachments at this age may be related to babies' developing cognitive (thinking) skills. At this age, babies show that they understand that an object exists, even if they cannot see it. This is called **object permanence**.

Children will use their attachment figure as a safe base from which to explore the world. A child will explore their environment but never stray far from their mother, making frequent trips back to 'base' before venturing out on another exploration.

Two distinct behaviour patterns are seen in this stage.

- **Social referencing**: when confronted with a new situation babies of about 10 months will look at their mother's face to check their expression. They are able to tell, by their mother's response, whether or not the situation is safe or something to be feared.

In a new situation, a baby will turn to look at her mother's face and reads her expression to see if the situation is safe

- **Separation protest** and fear of strangers: this can start as early as 5 months and can continue in intensity until about 16 months, when the behaviour starts to gradually decline. Summarising the research from several studies, Helen Bee (1995) suggests that children who are general fearful about new situations tend to show more fear of strangers than other children. Bee also suggests that children who have experienced an upheaval in their life such as the birth of a sibling, resulting in separation from the mother, may show more fear of strangers.

4 Multiple attachments

The age when babies begin to form strong attachments to more than one or two adults varies considerably from child to child. Some children form strong attachments to more than one adult from the beginning, particularly if they have close contact with family members or a regular care giver such as a key worker. Other children form a strong attachment to their mother first and only later, around 18 months, form attachments to other adults such as relatives.

John Bowlby (1907–90) considered the mother to baby bond to be the most important relationship in a child's life because, usually, it is the mother who cares most for the child and is able to help the baby form the intense adult to baby attachments that are needed for the future wellbeing of the baby. Bowlby's work was misinterpreted to mean that the mother is the only person whom a baby can satisfactorily attach to. In fact babies can, and do, form satisfactory attachments with several care givers as long as these relationships are given time to develop. Bowlby's work is one of the reasons that we now think that it is important that babies being cared for in childcare establishments are looked after by as few adults as possible.

How do attachments occur?

There are many theories that try to explain how attachments occur. The four main approaches are:

- the biological approach which suggests that babies are born with the ability to form attachments and that the process is instinctive
- the behaviourist approach which suggests that babies learn who supplies their physical needs and want to be near that person
- the sensitive responsiveness theory which suggests that babies form attachments to those who are aware of the babies' social needs and interact with them
- the communication theory which suggests that babies do not want to be on their own and develop attachment behaviours to keep adults near them.

In reality, it is unlikely that any one process is dominant in the formation of attachments as there is likely to be a variety of mechanisms at work.

Different kinds of attachments

The quality of a child's attachments can vary in both **strength** and **security**.

Factors that may have an adverse effect on the strength and security of attachments
Factors include:

- family disruption such as moving house or the birth of a sibling
- adverse social conditions which stress the parents
- institutional care rather than family care
- rejection of a baby by a mother
- mothers who are depressed
- mothers who are inconsistent and/or unresponsive to the baby's needs
- factors affecting the baby's ability to respond to the parent or carer, for example ill or irritable babies, babies who cannot see or babies who have a severe learning disability.

37

Long-term effects

The results of the various studies (Ainsworth *et al.* 1978, Main and Solomon 1985) indicate that the quality of attachment children have to their parents/carers has a lasting effect, at least until school age when these studies were undertaken. But, of course, it does not mean that all children will be affected in the same way.

Table 2.1 Long-term effects of attachment

The securely attached child	The insecurely attached child
Is more popular with his or her peers.	Is more clingy to the teacher in the pre-school years and will attract attention by being 'naughty'.
Has higher self-esteem.	Has more temper tantrums and aggressive behaviour.
Is more flexible and resourceful.	Is more likely to have behaviour problems (boys only).
Is easier to manage in the classroom.	Can recognise themselves in a mirror earlier than a securely attached child.
Shows more empathy towards other children and does not show pleasure in other children's distress.	
Will socialise more freely with a stranger as a pre-schooler.	
Can concentrate for longer as a toddler and is a more effective problem solver.	
Between 18 and 30 months shows more mature and complex play.	

A child who is insecurely attached will be more clingy to the childcare practitioner in the pre-school years

---

✔ PROGRESS CHECK

1 Describe the two process involved in the attachment of an adult to a baby.
2 What might be the long-term effect on a baby of a mother who is inconsistent or unresponsive to her infant's needs?
3 Describe the stages in the process whereby a baby becomes attached to an adult.
4 Why is it important that a baby, being cared for during the day in a nursery, has a key worker?
5 What might lead you to suspect that a five-year-old boy in a reception class had an insecure attachment to his main carer?
6 Looking at your responses to question 5, can you suggest possible alternative reasons for this type of behaviour?

SEPARATION

Earlier in the chapter, it was noted that when a baby has become attached to a parent or carer they start to show separation protest. There has been considerable research undertaken into the effects, on a child, of being separated from someone to whom they are strongly attached.

The effects of separation

> **THINK ABOUT IT**
>
> What situations can you think of when babies or children are separated from their main parents or carers?

The stages that a child goes through when separated from a parent or carer have been extensively studied. In this country, James and Joyce Robertson in the 1960s and 1970s observed and filmed children who had been separated from their parents for a variety of reasons. Films included ones of a toddler in a residential nursery while his mother was in hospital and of a young girl in hospital without her mother. The work of the Robertsons led professionals to realise that children, whom it was previously assumed were coping well with separation, were, in reality, deeply distressed. The realisation that children in hospital were suffering from the effects of separation has led to considerable change in hospital practice. Now parents and carers are encouraged to stay with the hospitalised child and there are facilities for whole families to stay together whilst one child is being treated.

The stages that a child goes through when separated from a parent or a career are outlined below.

1 Protest: typical behaviour would include screaming and crying, clinging, kicking, struggling, and other behaviours designed to stop the parent/carer from leaving. The child will watch the door in anticipation of their parent's return. You can usually tell by the child's behaviour what the child is feeling.
2 Despair: the initial protest behaviour dies down and the child seems much calmer and resigned to the situation. The hurt and anger are still there, but these emotions are felt internally. To the casual observer the child may appear to be depressed and apathetic. The child may reject offers of

This child is protesting at being left with a baby sitter

comfort from other adults, preferring to comfort themselves by thumb sucking, rocking and so on. The child may stop watching for the return of the parent.

3 Detachment: after a while the child will appear to have adjusted to the situation. He will begin to make relationships with adults, but on a superficial level. If his mother returns he may ignore her or even reject her.

All children are individuals and not all children will show these stages. The behaviour shown by children may depend on the length of time they are left. If a child is left for an hour in a shopper's crèche he may still be in the protest stage when his mother comes to collect him. A child, who has had to go into emergency care for several days because of an illness to the mother, may pass through all of these stages.

Factors affecting the experience of separation

The age, gender and temperament of the child
Until babies are fully attached to their mothers/main carers at 7 months, they do not show much distress at being separated. From this age, until children are about 3 years, it is common for children to be distressed at being separated, with most distress being shown by toddlers between 12 and 18 months. Young children do not understand the concept of 'a few hours' or 'tomorrow' and may assume that their mother is never going to come back.

Boys tend to suffer more distress than girls and for both sexes' reactions to separation vary according to how easily children have made social relationships before the separation. Children who find social relationships difficult tend to suffer more effects of separation.

The previous experiences of the child

The more emotionally secure children are before the separation, the better they can cope. Children who have never been left, even for a very short time, may find their first separation very difficult. It has been found that children adjust better if they have had previous good experiences of separation. If a child has multiple attachments, this too will help them cope with separation.

Whether the separation is planned or unexpected

It is possible to prepare a children for a separation. If a child has to stay with his grandmother when a mother has a new baby, he can be prepared by staying with his grandmother for the occasional day, or overnight. Parents can also introduce him to role-play activities about staying with his grandmother. Unplanned separations are usually more traumatic because there is no possibility of preparing children and the situation is often surrounded by negative emotions that adversely affect them.

The consistent quality of the care that the child receives during the separation

Children separated from their main parents or carers will adjust better if the care they receive during the separation is of high quality. The most important feature is that the child needs to be looked after by as few people as possible so that they can begin to form a good relationship with another adult. For this reason, young children placed in the care of the social services are looked after by foster parents (as far as is possible) rather than in children's homes. Foster parents are able to provide more personal, family care than can be provided in group residential care. In nurseries and other childcare facilities, it is recommended that children are cared for by one key worker, rather than by several childcare practitioners.

Another important feature of the quality of care is that children need to be stimulated. Plenty of play activities and other experiences need to be organised as bored children find separation much more difficult to cope with.

The longer the period of separation, the more difficult it is for the child. Resent research indicates that emotional trauma in childhood can lead to deformities in critical parts of the brain.

The long-term effects of separation

Children who have negative experiences of separation can show long-term effects. These effects include:

- detachment behaviour where the children no longer seek a close relationship with their mother, as if they are scared she might go away again
- school phobia, when, it is thought, children fear something dreadful will happen to their mother while the children are at school
- the inability to make appropriate relationships when older.

Children may also show these effects as a result of other life events that have caused emotional trauma. For example, not every child who suffers from school phobia has experienced a separation. The child may have experienced bullying at school.

Helping children cope with separation

Childcare and education facilities

The number of mothers in employment who have very young children is on the increase. Some of these children will be cared for by relatives, childminders or nannies, but there is a rise in the numbers of very young children in childcare and education facilities. Concerns have been expressed that group care, especially in a child's first year, could disrupt infant to parent attachment. There has been a variety of studies into the effects on infants of being cared for by different people. Tony Munton (2001) has reviewed several studies and concludes that research 'does not support the view that healthy development depends on very young children being looked after by their mothers'. He describes a study by Judy Dunn, where she found that children, who were looked after by a number of different care givers, developed secure attachments as long as the carers knew the child well and could respond effectively to their needs. Most studies report similar findings, although Jay Belsky claims that there are findings to show that children under 1 year of age, who spend more than 20 to 30 hours a week being cared for by others, can become more aggressive and disobedient than children not exposed to this level of non-parental care. However, more recent evidence from a study undertaken by the National Institute for Child Health has found no such adverse effect. Munton concludes that, overall, there is evidence that young children can benefit from being cared for by others as long as that care is of good quality. Good quality childcare would ensure young children are cared for by as few adults as possible, with whom the children are able to form stable attachments. A good partnership between parents and children's childcare practitioners is essential if children are to settle well and benefit from attending a nursery.

Before a child starts attending a nursery, parents can:

- find out the establishment's policy about settling children in. This usually involves a gradual introduction over a few days so, if the parent is working, leave may have to be arranged

- get him used to separation by leaving him with close friends and family for short periods of time

- encourage close friends and family to involve themselves with him so that he has the opportunity of making multiple attachments

- if the child is old enough, use role play, books and other activities to help him understand what is going to happen

- try to introduce him to someone else who goes to the same nursery

- help the child pack his bag on the first day and let him take something belonging to one of the parents, such as a handkerchief, to look after so that he knows the parent is coming back

- get up early enough so that the day starts calmly

- stay with the child for the first few visits. Let him explore the nursery and come back to the parent as a safe base

- liaise with the child's key worker. Tell him or her the child's likes and dislikes, how he shows he is tired, the words he uses to make his needs known and if he uses a dummy or a comfort blanket

The key worker will need to know that this baby needs his dummy and his comfort blanket to go to sleep

- when they leave the child, tell the child that they are going. They should never just disappear. Parents should always tell the child when they are coming back.

When the child has started nursery, the establishment can:

- have a settling-in policy which encourages the parents to settle the children in gradually over a period of time, depending on the child
- use a key worker system
- ensure that there is plenty of time for the key worker to get to know the parent and child in a relaxed atmosphere
- ensure that the key worker always greets the child and the parent in the same way so that the child is soothed by familiar routine
- establish a routine at nursery for the child so that everyday activities such as nappy changing and mealtimes become familiar and predictable. Care routines are excellent opportunities for the key worker and the child to develop a satisfying, reciprocal relationship with each other
- ensure that the key worker keeps in close contact with the parents and tells them as much as possible about how the child spent his day
- maintain a good relationship with the child's parents/carers. Children are sensitive to the feelings of the adults around them and will be reluctant to settle if they feel that their mother is unhappy
- ask the parents/carers about any special needs that the child may have or any religious or cultural factors that will influence the child's care
- try to have welcome signs in the family's language, if the family's main language is not the language of the nursery, and consider the provision of an interpreter if needed. Make sure that the resources of the nursery reflect the child's family background in a positive way.

Preparing for a stay away from home without the parents or main carer

Depending on the age of the child, the preparation will be much the same, excepting in this case the child will be staying for a few days or longer. It is important that whoever is caring for the child knows all about bedtime routines, bathing and so on. Let the child pack his case if he is old enough. Let him select his favourite toys and comforters. Give him something belonging to his parents to look after. When the child is away, parents should telephone if possible or send cards every day.

The people looking after the child can:

- make sure that they know everything about the child's normal routine, likes and dislikes, and how the child communicates his needs
- try to keep to a daily routine that is similar to the one at home, as far as possible
- resist the temptation to be over-indulgent. Children feel secure if expectations for behaviour are the same as at home
- take the child to see the parent if at all possible
- keep talking to the child about the parent and encourage telephone calls and so on
- use books, activities and role play to help the child understand the situation
- recognise that the child may regress (go back to a younger way of behaving), so be prepared for a child who was previously clean and dry to have 'accidents'. Some children who have given up a dummy may ask for one again and children who have been happily sleeping without a night light for some time may need one
- have a photograph of the parent.

CASE STUDY

Jamie is 2 years old and lives with his mother in London. Jamie's father is no longer with the family and has no contact with them. Jamie's mother, Susan, is due to go into hospital for an operation on her leg. She will have to stay in hospital for five days but will be unable to look after Jamie for at least two weeks after the operation. Susan's mother lives fifty miles away. Ideally, she would have liked to care for Jamie in his own home but she has elderly relatives living with her and cannot leave them. It has been decided that the best thing would be for Jamie to stay with his Grandma for three weeks while Susan has her operation and recovers.

1 How can Jamie be prepared for this separation?
2 What could Jamie take with him to his grandmother's that might help him?
3 What behaviour might he show while with his grandmother?
4 How can Susan help while Jamie is away?
5 What behaviour might Jamie show on his return?

SPECIAL CASES INVOLVING SEPARATION

There are other reasons why children are separated from their parents and in this section we will briefly look at the effects of the death, divorce and the imprisonment of a parent.

Bereavement

Children commonly experience temporary loss in their lives. It may be when their mothers return to work and they are looked after by a childminder or in a nursery. Children may experience more substantial loss when family or close friends move away, they may experience loss when a pet dies. The death of a parent or sibling is the ultimate loss, but the way in which children are helped to come to terms with minor losses can affect the way they deal a bereavement.

It used to be considered that children should be shielded as far as possible from the reality of death. Children were not taken to funerals and often children were 'protected' from the grief of other family members in case they were upset. Now we realise that young children need to be treated with honesty and that they need to grieve as adults do.

Common reactions to death according to the age of the child

- Babies will suffer separation and loss reactions if their mother or main carer dies. If a sibling has died, babies will be affected by the emotions of their parents as well. They may be unsettled, lose weight, and have sleeping problems.

- Children between 1 and 3 years do not understand that death is permanent. They will ask when the person is coming back. They may think that something they did has caused them to go away. Some children will repeatedly search for the person who has died, or act out the situation with their toys.

- Children from 3 to 7 years are even more likely than the younger child to think that they were responsible for the death, especially if the adults around them avoid talking to them about it. When the parent or sibling was alive they may have had angry thoughts about them and perhaps wished them harm. After a death, the children may feel that their thoughts and wishes caused the tragedy. At this age children may seem to understand the permanence of death, only to reveal, later on, that they think that if they are 'very good' the person will come back. Some children will seem to accept the situation, only to ask sometime later, when their parent or sibling is going to come back. Repeated explanations may be needed until the child is in a position to understand fully. If children are not given the opportunity to talk, the effects of grieving are likely to be prolonged and the child could become emotionally disturbed.

The grieving process

Once a child fully understands the situation, the child may go into a period of shock. He may show the following reactions, depending on his age:

- 'mechanical' behaviour, that is carrying on as normal but lacking in spontaneity

- withdrawal, gazing into space for long periods
- signs of apprehension
- periods of panic.

Once the shock has worn off, children may show signs of separation anxiety such as:

- anxiety about being separated from family for any reason, for example refusing to go to school
- sleep problems
- regression to an earlier stage of development
- changes in eating habits, such as over eating as if they are trying to fill an empty hole, hoarding food and food refusal
- depression that may hide feelings of sadness and anger that they feel unable to express
- loss of concentration
- lower resistance to infection
- anxiety habits such as nail biting and hair twisting.

Children typically show symptoms of mourning for the first year following the death. Reactions are all very individual but can include denial, sadness and anger. Some children will be afraid to discuss their feelings with their family because they cannot face their parents' grief (family members may be experiencing similar reactions as the children). They may prefer to talk to someone outside the family. Others may want to talk only to family members.

When a parent dies, the children may experience two losses because the surviving parent is grieving and cannot give them the emotional help that they need. Similarly, if children lose a sibling, both parents may be grieving and unable to give time and attention to the surviving children. In these instances, it is important that children have an adult who is there for them alone, who can answer their questions honestly and help them through the grieving process. A warm and caring adult who is there for the child can also help the parents understand the child's behaviour at a time when they may find the needs of the surviving children difficult to deal with.

How childcare practitioners can help

It is inevitable at some time in the careers of childcare practitioners that they will be in the position of caring for a child who has suffered a bereavement. There are many useful organisations that can help with guidance and information. These can be found at the end of the book. Practical guidelines include the following.

- Spend time with the child and answer questions honestly. Be prepared to give explanations several times and do not be surprised if the child appears to understand one day and then ask a question another day that reveals that he has not fully come to terms with the situation. Be aware that the child may feel responsible for the death.
- The child may re-enact the death in his play. This is to be encouraged as it will help him understand what has happened. Encourage 'small world' play.

Small world play can help a child work through her emotions

- Depending on the age and maturity of the child suggest that he be allowed to attend the funeral, accompanied by an adult who is close to him, but not intensely grieving. All his questions about the funeral should be answered truthfully.

- Parents may need help and advice about financial matters, especially if the main wage earner has died. Be prepared to give them information about local agencies that can give advice and support after a bereavement.

Divorce and separation

Unfortunately, many children will experience the loss of a parent through divorce or separation. At the moment, it is usually the mother who is given custody of the children, with the father leaving the home to set up a different establishment. Most families have an arrangement where the father has access to the children some weekends and in the holidays. In some families, the children lose contact with their father altogether. The effects on the children depend on many factors, such as the age of the children, the children's gender, the relationship that the child had with the parent before the divorce, the relationship that the parents have after the divorce and the degree to which the child is subjected to poverty and domestic disruption.

Children in families where parents divorce experience three different kinds of stress.

1 In the period before the divorce there may be arguments and conflict between the parents. Parents may try to be 'civilised' in front of the children, hoping that the stress will not affect them too much. Children are very sensitive to atmosphere and may be adversely affected. Sometimes parents try to enlist the support of the children, who may feel that they have to take sides. Some parents are unable to contain their conflict and children may be witness to verbal and physical violence.

THINK ABOUT IT

Why do some children feel guilty or in some way responsible for their parent's divorce?

2 The news of the parents' decision to separate may be traumatic for the children and the family may undergo a period of disruption while decisions are made and new arrangements put in place. Children may feel anxious about where they will live and who will look after them.

3 After the separation, the children may experience separation anxiety and may grieve for the loss of the parent who has left. If the situation is handled sensitively, the children will gradually adjust to the new situation but if there is continuing conflict between parents then the children will continue to experience stress.

Reactions of children to the separation/divorce of their parents

- Short-term effects include defiance, negative attitudes and behaviour, anger, aggression, depression and guilt. School performance may go down and children may suffer an increase in illness.

- Children show different effects at different ages. Wallerstein and Kelly (1980) found that pre-school children show the most severe immediate effects. Typically, they regress to previous levels of behaviour and are often anxious and clingy. They worry about losing both parents and have a harder time adjusting to change than older children. Young children show fewer long-term effects than older children.

- There are long-term effects of divorce and separation on children. Research, summarised by Davenport (1996), indicates that children are more likely to leave home at the age of 16, due to friction in their home, than children from families where the parents have remained together. Children from separated families are also more likely to be married or living with someone by the age of twenty and to be parents themselves.

- Boys tend to be more affected than girls, especially if the father was absent before the boy's fifth birthday (Heatherington 1984, Tschann *et al.* 1987). In the short term, they show more distress and negative behaviour both in and out of school.

Factors that reduce the negative effects of divorce and separation

There is evidence that the long-term effects of divorce and separation on children is influenced by the way the parents communicate after the separation and the way access arrangements are organised.

- Children adjust best if they feel loved and that they are not a burden to the full-time parent. They are happy if that parent is seen to be coping well.

- Children need to continue frequent, positive contact with the part-time parent. They do not adjust very well if they are used as pawns in the parents' battles. It is important that parents speak and act positively about each other in front of the children.

- Children who see themselves as being financially worse off after the separation adjust less well.

- Adjustment is better if the child's lifestyle is not disrupted too much. Children adjust best if they continue to live in the same house and to go to the same school.

GOOD PRACTICE

Childcare practitioners can help children who are experiencing family breakdown by:

● encouraging them to talk about it. There are several books available which can be used with children to help them understand what is going on

● respecting the child's confidences. You may be given information that the parents would rather you didn't know.

● giving them opportunities to express their feelings, verbally and in play activities

● maintaining a familiar routine – this is important

● maintaining full communication between the childcare practitioner and the parent which is essential if the needs of the child are to be fully met.

There is a continuing debate as to whether it is more harmful for children to be looked after by parents who remain together but who are in a constant state of conflict, or whether they suffer more harm because the parents separate. Evidence from research indicates that children need not be harmed by divorce or separation so long as:

● they are involved in discussions

● they are not materially deprived

● they continue to have good relationships with both parents

● they are satisfied with access arrangements.

Of all these, it is the quality of the relationship the child has with their parents that is the best protector.

Helping a child come to terms with a family breakdown

Imprisonment of a parent

The effects on children of having a parent in prison depends on the individual circumstances of the family. If children's fathers are in prison, they will suffer a separation similar to that which they might experience if the parents divorced, although there are special factors that will make the experience especially difficult to adjust to. If children's mothers are in prison, the children may be looked after by their fathers or by other relatives, or they may have to be taken into care. Whatever the situation the children will have to adjust to the loss of their mother. Some women's prisons allow inmates to keep their babies with them up until the age of 9 or 18 months depending on the establishment.

Factors affecting children with parents in prison

- Children may need to adjust to being cared for by relatives or foster carers.

- Some women with children are arrested on entry to this country. Their children may have to be cared for by foster parents who cannot speak their language, do not know their customs and who may not be aware of their dietary or physical needs such as skin and hair care.

- If a father goes to prison, the children have to adjust to their loss. Their mother may be in distress and in financial difficulty. The mother may be too distressed to give the children the emotional support that they need.

- If the children's father is in prison, the mother sometimes tries to shield the children from the shame of the situation and may tell them that he is working abroad. When the truth eventually emerges, the children may feel betrayed. In addition she will not be able to take the children to visit their father.

- Very young children may be taken to see their father in prison without a suitable explanation as to what a prison is. They may be very upset by the atmosphere and the minimal contact that they are allowed. A few prisons have play facilities where parents can play with their children when they are brought in to see them, but this is not common.

- Children who know that a parent is in prison should be allowed to visit them. Often they will have fantasies about what prison is like and will be frightened. They need to be carefully prepared as to what to expect. The reality is unlikely to be as frightening as the fantasy.

How childcare practitioners can help

It is vital that the childcare practitioner maintains a professional, non-judgmental attitude. It is important that the child is not led to believe that because the parent is in prison that he or she is a 'bad' person, even though they may have done 'bad things'. It is especially important that the parent looking after the child feels that they can discuss the situation with the childcare practitioner, and they will not do this if the practitioner is negative.

The following suggestions may be helpful.

- Keep the image of the parent who is in prison alive for the child by asking about how they are and talking to the child about any visits that they have had.

- Just as one can help children explore the subject of hospitals or divorce, one can help children from about pre-school age to explore the subject of prisons and visiting someone there. Stories and self-made books can be used with groups of children and the sessions can be planned in a general way so that the other children in the class need not know that a class member has a parent in prison.

GOOD PRACTICE

Confidentiality is of vital importance. If a childcare practitioner becomes aware of a child who has a relative in prison, the practitioner must ensure that only the people whom the parent wants to know are informed.

- Encourage the child to engage in small world play. A farm or a zoo that has fences or cages can help children act through their fears and fantasies about imprisonment.

- Liaise with the parent who is looking after the child so that you know when a visit is coming up. The child may be very excited beforehand but may be sad and disappointed if the visit did not go as well as planned.

- Observe the child closely for signs that they may be emotionally traumatised by the events. Some children may have witnessed the arrest, some may have nightmares, some may expect to see their parent at any moment when you are aware that this is impossible.

CASE STUDY

Comfort is a childcare practitioner in an under-fives education centre in an inner city area. One of her key children, Ben, aged 3 years, is giving her some concern. Instead of being his normal, exuberant self, Ben has been coming to nursery looking pale and washed out. He has become very clingy, both to his mother when she drops him off in the morning, and to Comfort. Ben follows her around all day, not letting her out of his sight. In addition Ben has started wetting himself, after having achieved bladder control six months ago. Comfort recognises the signs that Ben is under stress and has a private word with his mother. Ben's mother is reluctant to talk at first but eventually tells Comfort that Ben witnessed his father being arrested and that he is now in prison, on remand.

1 How can Comfort structure Ben's day to help him with the physical manifestations of the stress he is under?
2 What activities and experiences can Comfort provide to help Ben understand what is happening?
3 What support can Comfort offer to Ben's mother?
4 Should Comfort tell her manager about the situation?

✔ PROGRESS CHECK

1 What are the likely effects on a baby of under one year of age of the baby's mother dying.
2 What are the likely effects on a seven-year-old of his or her two-year-old brother dying?
3 How can the key worker of a three-year-old girl help her come to terms with the death of her grandma?
4 How can childcare practitioners help children in their care adjust to a divorce in the family?

PARENTING STYLES

In the previous section, we have seen how the quality of a parent's/carer's interaction with an infant can affect that child's attachments and future behaviour. Other aspects of parenting also have a powerful influence on the way that children behave and in this section we will be looking at some of these influences.

Warmth

From our own experience we know that people have different personalities. Some people are warm and friendly and we enjoy being in their company, while other people can be more aggressive, hostile and cold. Of course the most warm and friendly person may lose their temper sometimes, but most people's behaviour is relatively consistent. Children growing up in a family where their parents are warm will have a very different experience from the child brought up where one or both carers show more negative feelings.

Maccoby (1980) describes the characteristics of parents who are at either end of the warmth/ hostility **continuum**.

Warm parents:

- care about their children
- express affection
- put the needs of their children first
- are interested and enthusiastic about their children's activities
- respond with sensitivity and empathy to their children's needs.

At the other extreme are some parents who are openly hostile towards their children.

Hostile parents:

- reject their children
- show by their behaviour or their words that they do not love their children or are not interested in them.

Children brought up by warm parents tend to be more securely attached in their first two years. The characteristics of securely attached children can be found earlier in this chapter. The warmth of parents also appears to have an influence on the levels of self-esteem in children (see Chapter 3 for more details about self-esteem). Children know that they are loved and that their parents think highly of them. This influences the way they feel about themselves. In addition, children with warm parents have been found to have higher IQs (**intelligence quotients**) when measured in pre-school and junior school.

Cultural variations in child rearing

The way that parents bring up their children varies according to the class, religion and culture of the family. Accepted child-rearing practices for one family may not be the same as those in another. Childcare practitioners need

DEFINITION

continuum a continuous measure or scale. At one end of a continuum, individuals have a lot of what is being measured. At the other end of the continuum, individuals have little of what is being measured

DEFINITION

intelligence quotient a measure of intelligence where children's performance in intelligence tests is compared with the performance of children of a similar age. An IQ of 100 indicates that a child is of average intelligence

THINK ABOUT IT

Try to explain why children with warm parents tend to have a higher IQ than children who have hostile parents.

to be aware that the way they were raised may be very different from the way that some of the children in their care are being raised.

Most childcare practitioners believe that they understand the 'right way' for parents to bring up children. Our ideas have been shaped, not only by our education and training in early years, but also by the society in which we were raised. This may lead to an unconscious assumption that western child-rearing practices are superior to child-rearing practices from other cultures. Cross-cultural studies appear to indicate that there is no universally accepted way to bring up a child. Cardwell, Clark and Meldrum (1996) suggest that child-rearing practices should be ' judged in relation to assisting children to adjust to their culture'. There will, inevitably, be disputes between people of different cultures about the 'right' way to bring up children. Childcare practitioners need to find out as much as they can about the culture and child-rearing practices of the families they work with so that they can better understand the behaviour of the children in their care.

Cross-cultural studies include the following.

- Scheper-Hughes (1992) described very harsh child-rearing styles among parents of deprived families in the north east of Brazil. Families live in extreme conditions of poverty and only about half of the children survive until the age of 5 years. In these conditions, parents give minimal care to the children who are sickly or have a developmental delay, giving more care and attention to children who are strong and developmentally advanced. By the time children are aged 5 years, they are expected to contribute to the family by scavenging or stealing if they are boys and by doing the chores if they are girls. These child-rearing styles reflect the need for families to survive in the extreme conditions in which they find themselves.

- Konner (1977) described how the Zhun-Twsai people in Botswana care for babies in such a way that they hardly ever cry. Babies are kept so close to their mothers that they can be breast fed, or cared for, at the first sign of distress.

- Kagan and Klein (1975) described how, in isolated villages in a mountainous region of Guatemala, children never left the family home which was often a small, poorly lit, single room. This was because parents believed that the sun, dust and air outside were harmful for young babies. The infants were given very few playthings and were rarely talked to. Not surprisingly, at 1 year, infants scored poorly on developmental tests and were quiet and fearful. In their second year, children were allowed outside the home and very soon developed into active toddlers. Older children showed no developmental delay, showing that this extreme parenting style did not result in long-term difficulties.

There are many other, more general, examples where there are differences in child-rearing style between cultures. Some cultures expect boys and girls to take on different roles within the family. Some cultures, for example the Japanese, place great value on the development of close family relationships and the development of group identity. American child-rearing styles tend to emphasise independence, with less of an emphasis on group identity.

Dwivedi (1999) summarised western child-rearing practices as cherishing independence, with parents encouraging children to become independent as soon as possible, starting with separate sleeping arrangements for the baby. In contrast, within the Indian culture, dependability is cherished. In this culture there is an atmosphere of 'indulgence, physical closeness, common sleeping arrangements, immediate gratification of physical and emotional needs and a very prolonged babyhood so that the growing child deeply experiences the dependability of parents, extended family and the community' (Dwivedi 1999).

CASE STUDY

Ahmed is 4 years old and attends a nursery class in an inner city nursery school. At tidy up time Ahmed is seen to be standing, observing the other children putting away the toys, but not joining in. When asked why he isn't putting the toys away, Ahmed tells the childcare practitioner that tidying is for girls. He is a boy and won't do it. One of the adult helpers is overheard making a very negative comment about the way Ahmed has been brought up.

1 As Ahmed's key worker, how do you encourage him to tidy up?
2 How would you handle the situation with the adult helper?

PARENTAL CONTROL

All parents have to exert control over their children. At the most basic level parents need to control children so they are kept safe, but in addition to this children need to learn how to behave so that all members of the family can live together comfortably. The control that parents influence over children helps them learn the 'rules' of behaving in our society so that at school and as adults they can fit in and behave appropriately. This process is called socialisation, and although parents have a huge influence, there are other factors at work that affect this process.

Factors that influence the behaviour we think is appropriate

Every adult has an understanding of what behaviour is appropriate and what is not. Generally there is a degree of agreement within communities, for instance most of us would agree that we should not kill another human. However, on closer inspection, it is possible to think of exceptions to this. Most countries have an army that is expected to kill the nations' enemies. Some countries such as The Netherlands appear to be moving towards the idea that euthanasia is legal in specific situations and in Britain abortion is legal. Even within individuals our ideas about what is appropriate behaviour and what is not tends to change with experience, maturity and changing situations. Factors that influence the behaviour we consider appropriate include the following.

● The country we live in: every country has a set of laws that we must obey such as not stealing, paying our taxes and so on.

THINK ABOUT IT

Make a list of all the things that help a child learn what sort of behaviour is expected of them as adults.

- Our religion: most religions have a code that their followers adhere to that not only gives rules to live by, such as 'love thy neighbour' but may also give detailed instruction on what to wear and what to eat.

- Our culture: sometimes, when we meet someone from another culture, we may unwittingly offend them because of something we do, or do not do. An example of this would be when it is polite to give a belch after a meal in some cultures as recognition of having eaten well, whereas in other cultures this would be considered very bad manners indeed.

- Our social class: the way we talk and behave is influenced by our social class. We may feel uncomfortable if we are mixing with people from a different social class from us, in case we 'do the wrong thing'. These differences are probably not as pronounced as they were in the past.

- Our family: each family has a set of expectations about how family members should behave, which is based on the factors outlined previously but is also influenced by the way the parents themselves were raised.

How parents control their children

There are four aspects to consider when looking at how parents control their children:

- how clear rules are and how consistently they are applied
- how the parents want the children to behave
- parenting style
- methods of helping children behave appropriately.

Clear and consistent rules

For children to obey the rules of the family they need to understand them. Any rules need to be very clear so that there is no room for misunderstanding. The rules also have to be consistent. If there is a rule about not eating sweets between meals then this has to be applied by all adults in the home, every day. If a parent changes the rule because the children are whining, then the next time the children want sweets they will try the same tactic. This is an example of partial reinforcement which is described in more detail in Chapter 1. Inconsistent rules can lead to children who do not readily accept **discipline**, and who show a variety of behaviours to get the adult to change their minds.

DEFINITION

discipline the process of helping children learn appropriate behaviour

Some readers may automatically associate discipline with punishment, but the term is wider than this. In this book, the term is used to include positive behaviour management techniques such as the use of praise and rewards and clear explanations of expected behaviour as well as the use of punishment.

The techniques used to help children learn appropriate behaviour is commonly referred to as applying discipline.

How the parents want the children to behave

Parents all have different expectations of how they want their children to behave. Some parents have 'high' expectations of their children and expect them to take responsibility for aspects of their lives and to contribute to the overall running of the household. Of course, it is unrealistic to expect a three-

TRY THIS!

Either on your own or in small groups make a list of all the types of behaviour young children exhibit when they are trying to get an adult to change their mind about something. Using your own experience, what are the adult's emotions when being subjected to such behaviour.

A five-year-old can be expected to help get things ready for school the next day

year-old to do the housework, but they can tidy up their toys at the end of the day. A five-year-old can help get their things ready for school the next day and can lay the table for meals. Research has shown that children who are expected to be independent and helpful will have high self-esteem and be less aggressive and more caring towards others.

Parenting style

In the previous section, the warmth/hostility continuum was discussed. Another attribute that can be described as a continuum is how restrictive or permissive parents are. Restrictive parents, as described by Barnard, Bee and Hammond (1984) are those who have a lot of rules that the children have to obey. Many of the rules will be to do with keeping the children safe. Permissive parents have few rules and seem to be able to tolerate a higher degree of risk. A restrictive parent will give a child very little freedom and they will keep the child where they can see them at all times. Children of these parents will be the last in their class to be able to cross the road on their own, go to shops on their own, travel on public transport on their own. Restrictive parents also issue a lot of commands, and they tend not to explain why they want a child to behave in a certain way, expecting a child to obey just because a parent has told them too.

Permissive parents issue fewer commands and have fewer rules. These parents may take more time in explaining their decisions to their children and may encourage their children to explore and take more risks. However, permissiveness is sometimes a result of inconsistent parenting or neglect.

The most effective parents are those who are neither too restrictive, nor too permissive. Children are given freedom to make some decisions for themselves and explore, but within safe limits. Rules are consistently applied and the reasons for them are explained to the children. Such children are more likely to grow up with a high self-esteem, achieve more and are more independent than children with very restrictive or permissive parents.

Braummind (1984) has developed a description of the main parenting styles which takes account of both the warmth–hostility continuum and the permissive–restrictive continuum. This model identifies three main parenting styles, the authoritarian, permissive and authoritative styles. This model has been used as a model for much further research.

- Authoritarian style: a style that involves strict discipline with children being expected to follow the rules with no opportunity for children to negotiate. Harsh methods of punishment may be used (Glasgow *et al.*, 1997). Children subjected to this parenting style may be discontented, withdrawn and distrustful.

- Permissive style: permissive parents do not impose much discipline. The children are left to regulate their own behaviour. Studies have shown that children of permissive parents tend to be immature, impulsive and lacking in self-reliance. Maccoby and Martin (1984) made a further distinction, dividing permissive parents into indulgent parents who are warm and responsive towards their children and neglectful parents who are not responsive to their children, often fail to keep track of their whereabouts and do not get involved in their interests.

- Authoritative style: these parents are neither too authoritarian nor too permissive. They exercise control over their children's behaviour but also encourage children to be individuals. Parents listen to what the children have to say. Authoritative parents expect their children to behave in a mature way and help children achieve this by setting clear standards and by using non-punitive methods of discipline (Glasgow *et al.*, 1997) Children of such parents have been found to have high levels of self-esteem and tend to achieve better at school, than children raised by parents with other parenting styles.

Methods of helping children behave appropriately

The research on parenting styles has shown how important it is that parents use appropriate methods to guide their children's behaviour.

Some of you will remember being punished. For instance you may have been told off, have had to go without a treat or were sent to bed early. Some of you may remember being smacked. Others may have remembered more positive ways that were used to help you behave appropriately, for instance you may have been rewarded for good behaviour.

The process of helping children behave in ways that adults consider to be appropriate is often referred to as disciplining children.

Most children will need to be disciplined at some stage of their lives, but discipline that is too harsh, inappropriate for the child's stage of development or is humiliating and damages the child's self-esteem can lead to long-term negative effects.

Children who are too harshly disciplined may:

- appear too good or too quiet and be unable to express negative feelings
- be too sensitive to even mild criticism

TRY THIS!

In a small group think back to your childhoods and make a list of the ways that your parents guided your behaviour.

- fail to test their parent's authority in ways that are expected, for example temper tantrums are expected in a two-year-old
- have no sense of humour or joy in life
- be irritable and anxious most of the time
- show symptoms of stress in other areas such as feeding, sleeping and toileting
- learn to be aggressive as a response to parent's aggression.

There is considerable debate among parents and childcare and education practitioners as to which methods of controlling children's behaviour are acceptable. Most people would agree that beating a child hard enough to leave a mark is unacceptable, but many parents still think that an occasional smack is appropriate. Several countries have passed legislation to prevent parents from smacking their children, on the basis that since it is an offence to hit an adult, it should be an offence to hit a child. In addition, research into the effectiveness of punishment, outlined in Chapter 1, has shown that punishment is not the most effective method of controlling behaviour and that children respond best to positive approaches.

Why is it that parents still continue to use physical methods of punishment? Recent research, aimed at trying to understand why some parents are violent towards their children, recognises that there is often more than one factor at work. Factors that have been identified include:

- upbringing – if parents are smacked as children they are likely to repeat this behaviour with their own children
- culture – hitting children is more acceptable within some cultures than others
- level of education – the more educated parents are, the less likely they are to resort to physical methods of punishment. For instance, many child care and education students have changed their minds on this issue since they started their training
- stress, including poverty, job dissatisfaction and marital breakdown – parents are much more likely to hit their children if they are stressed or harassed
- alcohol/drugs – parents under the influence of alcohol and some drugs may become violent towards their children
- the personality/psychological makeup of the parent – some parents may be predisposed towards being violent because of their inability to control their anger
- factors to do with the child – some children may be more at risk of being hit by their parents than others, including children with behavioural difficulties, those with special educational needs and children who are severely disabled and need a great deal of care.

In Chapter 3 we will be looking at appropriate ways that childcare practitioners can use for controlling children's behaviour. A similar approach can be successfully adopted by parents.

1 Parents should understand that at certain stages of development, children show aggressive behaviour and that excessive reactions can strengthen the behaviour. For example, babies will often pull a parent's hair.

2 Fit the method of discipline to the child's stage of development. For infants and toddlers it is more appropriate to divert their attention to a more appropriate activity. If this fails to work parents may need to remove the child from the situation. Parents should always explain why they are acting in this way. From the age of 2 years, children can be helped by parents to understand why they did what they did. If a child wants a toy very badly and hits another child, parents could explain that they know how much the child wanted that toy and how she must have felt very out of control inside. Parents could then go on to say that the child mustn't hit other children and attract the child's attention in another direction.

3 Fit the method of discipline to the child. A very sensitive, shy child will need much more gentle handling than an extrovert, active child. A method of discipline that will be very effective for one child may have no effect on another.

4 When children are with other children, try not to intrude on how they are getting on with each other. There may be a point at which parents need to intervene, but part of growing up is learning how to sort out conflict situations.

5 Be a good role model for children. If parents yell or hit the children when they have done something wrong, they will learn that this is the appropriate way to behave.

6 When all the emotions have died down, talk to children about what happened and help them understand how the situation arose and how they might deal with it more appropriately next time.

7 After an incident when parents have had to discipline a child, they should comfort them afterwards. Give them the message that they are loved, but that they should not behave in this particular way.

Let the child know that you love him, but dislike his behaviour

8 Ask for children's ideas as to the best way of helping them change their behaviour. If it is reasonable, try it out next time and if it works tell them how clever they were.

9 If parents' methods of disciplining aren't working, they should think about the situation and try a new approach. There is little advantage carrying on with something that is ineffective.

10 Never use physical punishment. All it tells children is that parents have lost control and that it is appropriate to use physical aggression when one is angry.

KEY TERMS

You need to know the meaning of the following words and phrases. Go back through the chapter to make sure you understand them:

attachment
bonding
continuum
discipline
key worker system
separation protest
social referencing
security of an attachment
strength of an attachment

✔ PROGRESS CHECK

1 Describe the characteristics of a warm parent.

2 What advice could you give to the mother of a two-year-old boy who frequently snatches the toys of other children?

3 Why is it inappropriate to use physical methods of punishment?

4 Why do some parents use physical methods?

5 What type of parent is one who is very restrictive and controlling towards their children and at the same time is unresponsive to the children's needs?

6 What sort of long-term behaviour effects might you see in children raised by permissive parents?

FURTHER READING

Cardwell, M., Clark, L. and Meldrum M. (1996) *Psychology for A Level*, Collins Educational

This book contains a useful section on cross-cultural child-rearing practices (see Chapter 17) and is suitable for students studying at Level 3 and above.

Lindon, J. (2000) *Helping Babies and Toddlers Learn: A Guide to Good Practice with the Under Threes*, The National Early Years Network

This book contains good advice for childcare practitioners who are looking after very young children, with an emphasis on quality. It is suitable for students at all levels.

Munton, T. (2001) 'First choice' in *Nursery World*, page 10, 18 January 2001

This article gives a good overview of research into the effects on infants of being cared for by people other than their parents. It is suitable for students at all levels.

The National Council for One Parent Families (1991) *We Don't All Live with Mum and Dad: A Guide to Books for Children and Young Adults Living in One Parent Families*, The National Council for One Parent Families

Wells, R. (1997) *Helping Children Cope with Divorce,* Sheldon Press

This is a useful practical guide for anyone who is supporting children in this situation.

Woodhead, M., Faulkner, D. and Littlejohn, K. (eds) *Cultural Worlds of Early Childhood*, Routledge in association with The Open University

Cultural differences in child-rearing styles are discussed by Michael Cole in Chapter 1 of this book, which is suitable for students studying at Level 4.

These three general texts have good sections on attachment and separation.
Bee. H. (1995) *The Developing Child*, Longman
    This book is suitable for students studying at Level 4.
Davenport, G.C. (1996) *An Introduction to Child Development*, Collins Educational
    This book is suitable for students studying at Level 2 and Level 3.
Flanagan, C. (1996) *Applying Psychology to Early Child Development*, Hodder and Stoughton
    This book is suitable for students studying at Level 2 and Level 3.

These two books contain good, practical information and will be appropriate for students on all courses.
Berry Brazelton, T. (1992) *Your Child's Emotional and Behavioural Development: The Essential Family Reference Book*, Penguin Books
Leach, P. (ed.) (1992) *Young Children Under Stress Starting Points: 13 Practical Guides for Early Years Workers*, The National Early Years Network

These two books are 'classics' and will be of interest for students on Level 3 and Level 4 courses.
Bowlby, J. (reprinted 1990) *Child Care and the Growth of Love*, Penguin Books
Robertson, J. and Robertson, J. (1989) *Separation and the Very Young*, Free Association Books

These are useful books about bereavement in childhood.
Farrant, A. (1998) *Sibling Bereavement: Helping Children Cope with Loss,* Cassell
Lindsay, B. and Elsegood, J. (1996) *Working with Children in Grief and Loss*, Baillière Tindall
Pennells, S.M. and Smith, S. (1995) *The Long Forgotten Mourners: Working with Children,* Jessica Kingsley

These are written for children about bereavement.
Burningham, J. (1988) *Granpa*, Cape
Reuter, E. *Christopher's Song*, Hutchinson
Someone Special Has Died, St Christopher's Hospice

These are useful insights into the problems of children who have parents in prison.
Blake, J. (1990) S*entenced by Association,* Save the Children
Lloyd, E. (ed.) (1992) *Children Visiting Holloway Prison*, Save the Children
Shaw. R. (1992) *Prisoners' Children: What are the Issues?,* Hodder and Stoughton

CHAPTER 3

Identity

This chapter includes:

- The self-concept
- Gender identity
- Ethnic identity.

Most of us find it relatively easy to describe ourselves to others. Our descriptions would include physical characteristics such as age, gender, hair and skin colour and our height and weight. We would probably describe our personality characteristics such as whether or not we are shy or outgoing. Our description might also include the various roles we play. We may describe ourselves as a parent, a student or a childcare practitioner. By the time we reach adulthood we usually have a good idea of who we are, a sense of identity. Some people grow up to have a strong, positive sense of identity. They feel good about themselves, are confident of their abilities and have a clear sense of where they fit into society. Some people grow up to be less positive about themselves, they may not feel so confident about what they can do and are uncertain about their role in society. How we feel about ourselves and our sense of identity has a profound effect on our behaviour. If we feel strong and capable we will be much more likely to take on new challenges, and are much likely to succeed than individuals who feel that they have few skills and little to offer. Whether or not we grow up to believe in ourselves depends on social and cultural factors such as the effects of our upbringing and experiences we have encountered since birth. In this chapter, we will be investigating how children develop a sense of identity and how this can affect behaviour.

THE SELF-CONCEPT

When we look in the mirror and see ourselves we see not only a face, but a person whom we know better than anyone else. We know what we look like, our hopes and dreams, the views we hold on different subjects, the relationships we have with others and the roles we play. Our **self-concept** is influenced by value judgments we make about ourselves. For example, do we like who we see in the mirror or are there aspects of ourselves that we do not like or about which we feel ashamed? The knowledge and attitudes we have about ourselves is gained over a lifetime of experience and is called our self-concept.

The self-concept has three different parts:

- **self-image**
- self-esteem
- ideal self.

Self-image

When researchers have asked similar questions to the 'Try This!' exercise they generally find out that responses can be divided into four general categories.

1. Personality traits such as extrovert, cheerful, shy, or even tempered.
2. Social roles which would include:
   - descriptions of employment such as student, childcare practitioner or teacher
   - family roles such as mother, father, sister or son
   - descriptions of roles to do with leisure activities or community involvement, such as football player or councillor.
3. Physical characteristics such as age, gender, height, weight and skin colour.
4. Culture, ethnic background, religion and class.
   People's descriptions of themselves vary according to the circumstances they are in. If you are the only male in a group you would be more likely to use gender in your description. In a similar way, if you are the only person of your culture in a group you would be more likely mention this.

Ideal self

This is the person we would like to be. We all have different ideal selves depending on the way we have been brought up, cultural and religious influences, and events in our lives. If our parents highly valued academic excellence and sporting ability, our **ideal self** might include being an academic success and an accomplished sports person. Society puts a high value on attractiveness and our ideal self might include factors such as being the correct weight for our height and being good looking.

If, while we are growing up, we see that people who are disabled or who are from minority groups are discriminated against, our ideal self is likely to include being 'able bodied' and from a majority group.

Self-esteem

This is the value judgment about the way we see ourselves (our self-concept). It is influenced by how close our self-concept comes to our ideal self. In

---

DEFINITION

self-concept the mental picture that individuals have about themselves

DEFINITION

self-image how we would describe our selves

TRY THIS!

Ask a small group of adults to write down a description of themselves. Compare the descriptions. Are there any similarities in the way that people have described themselves? Some descriptions may relate to appearance, others to personality characteristics. What other sorts of descriptions have been used?

DEFINITION

ideal self a description of what we would like to be

THINK ABOUT IT

If it is perceived that society does not value people who are disabled or who are from a minority ethnic group, how might that affect an individual's ideal self?

On the day of their degree ceremony these young women are likely to describe themselves as graduates

DEFINITION

self-esteem   the evaluations we make about ourselves. Individuals who think positively about themselves are said to have high self-esteem. Individuals who think negatively about themselves are said to have low self-esteem

general, the closer our self-concept is to our ideal-self, the higher will be our **self-esteem**.

The level of self-esteem that children have has a direct effect on their behaviour. Children who believe that they are not valued, are unattractive or inadequate in some area will tend to behave in ways that confirm these expectations. Children with low self-esteem tend to give up on tasks easily because they 'know' that they cannot succeed. They may behave in inappropriate ways because they think it is expected of them because they are the 'naughty' ones in the class.

Leon Feinstein (2000) and his research team from the London School of Economics have recently reported on some of the results of a thirty-year study looking at all children born in the first week of April 1970 (The British Cohort Study). The research team found that boys who were recorded as having a low self-esteem at the age of 10 years were more likely to be unemployed as adults. Children with similar levels of academic achievement at 10 years of age were likely to earn more as adults if they had high levels of self-esteem as children.

The dimensions of self-esteem
Jillian Rodd (1996) describes three dimensions of self-esteem:

- competence
- control
- worth and significance.

1 Competence: young children need to feel competent and successful and have a natural drive to learn new skills and become increasingly independent.

They are limited by their age, size and stage of development. Sometimes children or adults may have unrealistic ideas about what the children can achieve. Failure will lead to frustration and the child who repeatedly fails will begin to develop negative ideas about their competence.

2 Control: part of our feelings of self-esteem lie in the extent to which we feel in control of situations. Young children also need to feel that they have some measure of control over what happens to them.

3 Worth and significance: children need to feel accepted, loved and respected by those around them. Without these feelings of worth and significance, children will grow up to have low self-esteem. After all, it is very difficult to feel good about yourself if you feel unloved and rejected by others.

CASE STUDY

Maria is a student on a Childcare and Education course. It is her second year and she has just started a training placement in a private day nursery. Maria is upset at the way that two of the unqualified staff treat the children. They often seem to be shouting at the children and telling them off. They have obvious favourites and she heard one of them telling a boy, 'I'm fed up with you, you never do anything right. Why can't you be good like Amy?' One child, Ade, is often left to wander around the nursery, crying and whining. Once, when Maria went to comfort Ade, one of the staff told her to leave Ade alone because Ade was only trying to get attention and that nothing was really wrong with her.

1 What are the possible effects on Ade and the other children of the staff's behaviour?
2 What is the best course of action for Maria to take?

Raising children's self-esteem in childcare and education settings

The following guidelines are based on the need to help children feel competent, in control and significant within early years settings.

- Childcare practitioners should set realistic challenges for children and help children set realistic goals for themselves.

- Break down complicated activities for children into small tasks and give the child strategies which will help them complete the task.

- Encourage independence by letting children complete tasks for themselves, such as dressing, even if it would be quicker to do it for them.

- Mistakes are all part of learning. If children make mistakes point out ways to avoid the mistake the next time. If children are disciplined too harshly for making mistakes they may stop trying to tackle challenging tasks.

- Do not just praise success, but also give positive feedback to children who are putting a lot of effort into completing tasks and are improving their skills. If children are not successful this time, let them know that they will get there eventually. You could say something like 'Doing up shoe laces is very difficult. You have tried so hard. With a bit more practice you will manage it.'

Encourage children to dress themselves

- If children are getting disheartened about learning a new skill, point out to them things they have succeeded in doing in the past. You could say something like 'I know you are cross that you cannot tie your shoe lace up at the moment. Do you remember how cross you got when you were learning how to do up your zipper? But you can do that fine now'.

- Avoid competition and comparisons with others, instead encourage children to try to improve on their own previous accomplishments.

- Encourage children to praise themselves so that they do not have to rely on others to give them approval. Let children hear you praise yourself when things go well.

- Wherever possible, provide children with a range of activities so they can choose what they want to do.

- Encourage children to make decisions. Decision making needs to be scaffolded. You might ask a two-year-old whether they want to wear the tee shirt with the flower on it or the tee shirt with the gold bits. As children get older you can give them more choice. You could ask them to go to the drawer and get the clothes they want to wear for the day.

- Have a predictable routine to the day. Children who can anticipate what happens next will feel in control.

- Be consistent about discipline. All children should know what is expected of them. See Chapter 4 for more detail.

- Children and their families should be respected.

- Make sure you do not have favourites.

- Include all children in activities.

- Use positive behavioural management techniques, discussed in Chapter 4.

- Foster an environment where children feel loved and secure and can trust adults.
- Make sure that activities and resources within the nursery reflect all children in a positive light. Children who use a wheelchair should be able hear stories where the hero/heroine uses a wheelchair. Posters and books should contain positive images of children and adults from a variety of ethnic backgrounds, cultures and religions. This topic will be looked at in more detail later in this chapter.
- Always be encouraging, never tell children they are silly or stupid.
- Never shout at children.
- Let the children know, by your words and actions, that you enjoy their company.

Factors that influence the development of the self-concept

In describing the components of the self-concept we have already looked at some of the factors that influence its development. According to Michael Argyle (1969) these factors can be divided into four categories:

- the reaction of others
- comparison with others
- social roles
- identification.

The reaction of others

There has been a variety of experiments that show that how we rate ourselves for a particular activity or characteristic is influenced by our knowledge of how others have rated us. In addition there is evidence that indicates that our behaviour will change to match our self-image. Some experiments conducted in the past would be considered unethical today, but most experiments follow the same general pattern:

- participants are asked to rate themselves on a particular task
- a so called 'expert' gives participants a rating of their performances, which unknown to the participants, is unrelated to their actual performance levels
- participants are asked to rate their performances again
- participants are asked to repeat their performance.

In general, it is found that if individuals are rated highly, their self-ratings increase, whilst negative ratings by the 'experts' will lead to depressed self-ratings. In addition, it is a common finding that actual levels of performance change to reflect the new self-ratings.

Sometimes the views of 'experts' can affect an individual's self-concept indirectly. In a classic experiment by Rosenthal (1966) it was shown that adult expectations have a direct effect on children's achievement. A teacher, who was taking over a new class, was told that within the class there was a group of children whom experts had predicted would make rapid intellectual growth as measured by their IQ scores. The rest of the class were expected to progress as usual throughout the year. In reality, the group of children were

THINK ABOUT IT

This research study raises ethical issues and nowadays permission is unlikely to be given for such an experiment. The teacher, children and the children's parents were not aware of the true nature of the study.

1 Should the children have been used in this way?
2 Should the teacher have been used in this way?

chosen at random and were no different from the other children. At the end of the school year, the children were tested and, indeed the 'special' group had made more rapid development than the other children. It appears that the teacher had raised expectations of the children's abilities. These expectations may have led the teacher to expect more from the children, perhaps setting them more challenging tasks, giving them more attention and rating them more highly than the other children. The 'special' group of children would realise that the teacher had high expectations of them and their self-esteem would be raised. This in turn would have led them to feel confident of their abilities, which had a direct, positive effect on their learning.

Some of you may feel that no one was harmed during this study. Some of you may feel that the teacher was, unknowingly, manipulated into giving preferential treatment to one group of children and that the others were, perhaps, given less attention.

Young children only have the reactions of those around them to help them make self-judgments. If children are told by their parents that they are good looking, clever and a joy to be with, children will incorporate these views into their self image. At first, the children are influenced by the views of their parents then, as they grow older, they will be influenced by the opinions of other family members, childcare practitioners and teachers.

Splendid! You are clever. You have really worked hard today

In a study by Coopersmith in the 1960s, a group of boys with high self-esteem was compared with a group of boys with low self-esteem. Coopersmith found that the two sets of boys had parents who used significantly different child-rearing styles. Parents of the boys with high self-esteem appeared to have parenting styles very similar to the advice about raising children's self-esteem in childcare and education establishments outlined earlier. The boys with high self-esteem did better in school and continued to be more successful when they were adult than the boys with low self-esteem, even though, as children there was no difference in intelligence between the two groups.

Helen Bee (1995) has summarised the findings of several studies investigating parenting style. She concludes that children with authoritarian parents are likely to have lower self-esteem than children from other types of family. Authoritarian parents put high demands onto their children and are very controlling. At the same time there is a lack of warmth within the family and parents do not respond well to their children's needs. Parenting styles are looked at in more detail in Chapter 2.

Other negative parental influences on children's self-esteem may include:

- parents who do not encourage their children
- parents who feel resentful of the demands that parenting places upon them. These feelings can be transmitted to the children
- parents who make the children feel that they are responsible for their parents' levels of stress or tiredness
- children who perceive that their parents have no time for them.

Why do parents adopt negative parenting styles?

Throughout their careers, childcare practitioners will encounter parents whose parenting styles appear to be having a negative affect on their children and occasionally a childcare practitioner may need to discuss these issues with a child's parents. Discussion may reveal that parents are treating their children in the same way that they were treated as children. We begin to learn how to be parents by watching how our parents treated us. If parents' own experiences as children were negative, they are likely to repeat this pattern with their own children. Most parents do have their children's best interests at heart and may be unaware of the emotional damage they are doing. They may feel that they have strong moral or religious grounds for behaving as they do. Some parents are unaware of the effects of their behaviour on their children because they are preoccupied with dealing with overwhelmingly stressful situations or are affected by illness or the misuse of drugs and alcohol. Occasionally it may be necessary for a childcare practitioner to refer families to other professionals such as social services so that appropriate support can be given. In extreme cases it may become a child protection issue. Child protection is discussed in more detail in Chapter 4.

Comparison with others

Much of our self-image is the result of comparing ourselves with others. If we think of ourselves as tall or short or fat or thin we are comparing ourselves with other people. From the moment we are born, our parents and families start comparing us with other children. Sometimes this has a negative effect. If parents are constantly comparing a child unfavorably with a brother or a sister, the child is likely to grow up with very low self-esteem. Parents and childcare practitioners should avoid comparing brothers and sisters. Instead it is better to concentrate on the different abilities that the children have. Once children reach school, they start comparing themselves with others, not only in academic ability but also sporting prowess or how popular or how attractive they are. It is not possible to stop this happening but adults can help by minimising

> **TRY THIS!**
>
> Look at the suggestions for promoting children's feelings of self-esteem in childcare and education establishments outlined earlier on in this chapter (pages 65–67). Use this information to make a leaflet or a poster which could be used as a guide for parents.

competition and comparisons in the classroom, especially when children are very young. Children who experience negative reactions from others because of their ability, race, religion, culture or class will internalise these negative reactions and may develop feelings of low self-esteem. There are higher levels of antisocial behaviour in working-class young people, who have been shown to have lower self-esteem (in general) than children from middle-class backgrounds. It is thought that antisocial behaviour may be a way of hitting out at the values of a society that often makes working-class children feel inferior.

CASE STUDY

Simon is 7 years old and lives with his parents and brother Josh, who is eighteen months older than him. Because of their birthdays, Simon is only a year behind Josh in school, Josh being one of the oldest in his class and Simon being one of the youngest. Josh has always achieved well at school. He started talking early and was reading simple books before he started school. The family value academic excellence very highly with both parents having professional jobs. Simon has always been in Josh's shadow. Because he is a stocky child and he is almost the same height as Josh and friends and family forget there is an eighteen-month age gap. Simon is always trying to keep up with Josh and gets upset when he cannot play football as well, or do the same skateboard tricks as Josh. Simon is finding schoolwork a struggle. Both his parents and teachers keep on telling him that he is not as bright as his brother. Whatever Simon does, he cannot seem to do anything as well as Josh. Simon is starting to be disruptive in class. He is a very sociable child with lots of friends and has become the class clown, to the detriment of his, and others' studies. Simon will do anything to avoid reading at school or home because he finds it difficult. The mother of one of Simon's friends has discovered that Simon loves music and spends most of the time he is at her house playing with their piano. He has a lovely voice and enjoys acting and he is often to be seen directing his friends in little plays in the playground.

1 Why is it likely that Simon is suffering from low self-esteem?
2 What effects is this having on his development?
3 How could this situation have been prevented?
4 What advice would you give to Simon's parents about raising Simon's self-esteem?
5 What could Simon's teachers do to help?

Social roles

Earlier on in the chapter, it was explained that part of an individual's self-image involves a description of their various roles. These roles include occupations, relationships and categories such as 'friend'. When we are very young, we have few roles. We are a daughter or a son, we may be a brother or a sister. As we grow older, we add more roles. We may be someone's friend, a 'Brownie', a footballer, a chorister or a class monitor. As we progress through the education, system we may be a pupil, student or graduate. Still later, we may describe ourselves by our occupation such as childcare practitioner, teacher or manager.

As children acquire new roles, their self-image adjusts to take account of this. At first, when taking on a new role, many of us feel that we are acting the part, but gradually we become used to the new role and it begins to feel natural. Some of you may remember starting college and for the first time took on the role of a student. This may have felt very strange at first, but soon you began to fit in and feel at home in your new role.

Identification

This is the process whereby individuals take on some of the qualities and ideas of someone else. In Chapter 1, it was discussed how young children identify with the parent of the same sex, that is they will copy what parents do and say. When we identify with someone strongly enough our self-image will change to reflect this. **Identification** is one of the processes involved in children developing a sense of gender identity.

DEFINITION

identification the process whereby individuals take on the qualities and ideas of others

Patterns in the development of the self-concept

Children develop a self-concept gradually. They are born unable to differentiate themselves from others. As children interact with their surroundings and are influenced by the social and cultural environment in which they are raised, they gradually develop self-awareness and their self-concept develops. There are no fixed stages in the development of the self-concept but there are general patterns that can be identified.

Newborn babies

When babies are born they do not have a self-concept because they cannot, yet, distinguish between themselves and others. If they see a hand they have yet to learn if it belongs to them or not. Over the next few months, babies learn to associate one experience with another. If they bite their mothers' hands, it won't hurt but, if they bite their own hands, they experience sensations of discomfort. Babies learn that if they cry, someone will pick them up and they also begin to associate the movement of their limbs with muscle sensations.

This baby is beginning to recognise herself in a mirror

Around 9 months to 18 months

By about 18 months, infants clearly demonstrate that they know they are separate beings, a process which begins to be demonstrated at around 9 months of age. One way of testing this is to put a spot of colour on a baby's nose. When the baby is placed in front of a mirror, if she touches the spot of colour on her own nose, it shows that she can recognise herself in the mirror.

Around 18 months to 2 years

Infants are able state their own name, and will use their name when they see images of themselves in mirrors or are shown photographs of themselves.

Pre-school children

By 2 years of age, most children have achieved **gender identity**, that is they can indicate that they know they are boys or girls.

Ethnic identity, the ability to describe yourself by ethnic group comes later and research has shown that it depends on the child's ethnic background. Research undertaken primarily in the USA and Canada indicates that most white children achieve this by 4 years of age, while black children achieve this somewhat later. Gender and ethnic identity are discussed later on in this chapter.

Infant school children

By the time children are 5 to 7 years old they are able to give good descriptions of themselves in physical terms. They can describe themselves in terms of hair colour, age, and size, as well as gender and, by the time they are 8 years, most children can describe themselves in terms of ethnic group. Children of this age will also describe themselves in terms of what they like to play with, where they live and what things they are good or bad at doing.

It is not until children are over 8 years that they really begin to compare themselves with others, or to describe themselves in less concrete terms such as beliefs, social skills and personality characteristics. The development of children's ideas about whom they are continue throughout childhood and adolescence. It is not usually until individuals are young adults that a relatively stable self-concept is achieved. Although, by adulthood, there is a degree of stability in a person's self-concept, an individual's beliefs and thoughts about themselves will change throughout adulthood and old age, according to life events and experiences.

DEFINITIONS

gender identity   children have achieved gender identity when they can label themselves as a girl or a boy

ethnic identity   children have achieved ethnic identity when they can label themselves according to the ethnic group to which they belong

THINK ABOUT IT

What common life events and experiences are adults likely to encounter which will change their self-concept?

✔ PROGRESS CHECK

1 Explain the differences between the self-concept, self-image and self-esteem.

2 What factors influence the development of self-esteem?

3 How can parents and childcare practitioners help children acquire high self-esteem?

4 How does self-esteem affect children's behaviour?

5 Outline the general pattern of development for the development of the self-concept in children.

GENDER IDENTITY

In the previous section, we looked at how children begin to think of themselves as separate individuals and acquire ideas about whom they are, what they are like and what they can do. In this section, we will be looking at a specific area of identity which is to do with how children learn that they are male or female, and how this affects their behaviour.

The development of the concept of gender

As children grow older they learn several things about gender:

- people can be divided into male and female
- they are a girl or a boy
- that people do not change from male to female
- boys and girls behave differently and have different roles.

Gender identity and gender stability

At around 15 to 18 months, children begin to notice the difference between boys and girls. By 2 years old children can identify themselves as being male or female. And by the ages of 2 years and 6 months or 3 years, most children can point out girls or boys from photographs when asked.

By about 4 years of age, most children have achieved the concept of **gender stability**. That is the understanding that you have the same gender throughout life.

Gender constancy

By 6 or 7 years, most children have the understanding that individuals' gender remains the same despite changes that make them look very different. They understand that a boy will remain a boy even if you put him in a skirt and let his hair grow long.

The development of concepts about sex-roles

Our society has clear ideas about the differences between the way in which men and women should behave. In our society, for example, we have the concept that women should enjoy caring for children.

Each society has a different understanding of how men and women behave and this understanding is known as the **sex-role concept**. In the last fifty years, society's views on how men and women should behave are slowly changing, but such beliefs are still widely held. Although we all hold a sex-role concept, most of us are able to see that these roles do not apply to everyone, that some men and women do not behave in ways that conform to their sex-role. There are some adults who hold very inflexible views. They are unable to see that not all individuals conform to commonly held views about how men and women behave, these individuals hold **sex-role stereotypes**. That is they do not see people as individuals with different ways of behaving, but will assume all men or women conform to the sex-role concept with **sex-role behaviour**. It is a sex-role stereotype to say that all women enjoy caring for children, since there are many women who do not enjoy caring for children at all. Young children usually hold stereotypical views on sex-roles

73

and it is not until they are more mature that they may acquire a, more flexible, sex-role concept.

The development of concepts about sex roles in children

- Pre-school children are able to identify what are 'girl' behaviours and what are 'boy' behaviours. Some children of this age may already think that it is wrong for children to behave like the opposite sex, but most are flexible. It is common to see little boys choosing to dress up in a pretty frock at nursery, or play with the dolls.

- Children between the ages of 5 and 6 years are more likely to hold sex-role stereotypes and most children hold strong stereotypes by the ages of 7 and 8. Children of this age are very bound by rules and what they know to be right or wrong. They apply what they have learned about sex-roles rigidly.

We will be firemen and you can be the nurse

- Children of 9 and 10 are becoming more flexible and less rigid. They have a sex-role concept which contains ideas about how males and females should behave, but are beginning to be able to see that there are exceptions. They begin to understand that boys can play with dolls if they want to.

Sex-role behaviour

The development of sex-role behaviour

- Three- to four-year-old children can be observed in behaviour that reflects sex-role stereotypes. That is little girls can be found in the home corner, engaged in domestic play, while little boys prefer playing with action toys such as cars and trucks.

TRY THIS!

Observe a group of three-year-olds and record the toys that the children are playing with and the activities that they choose to join in with. Do boys and girls choose to play with different things?

As children grow older they begin to choose same sex friends to play with

- At this age, children begin to choose same sex friends to play with, a trend which increases as children grow older.

- Children in infant school take more notice of the behaviour of same sex children than of children of the other sex or adults. Toys for this age group are often strongly marketed as being girls' toys or boys' toys and it is unusual for children of this age to play with a toy designed for the opposite sex.

How do children acquire sex-role concepts and sex-role behaviour?

There is a variety of theories as to how children develop a concept of sex-role. These theories are based on the theories outlined in Chapter 1, about how children acquire behaviour. In summary:

- there is a biological influence, although most sex-role behaviour is learned

- parents and other adults reward appropriate behaviour

- children copy appropriate behaviour from others; they see behaviour modelled on the TV and in other media

- children use their cognitive (thought) processes and actively search out evidence to confirm or disprove schema they have about sex-roles. Children seek out information by observing other children and adults and by looking at pictures, books and television. They use this information to prove or disprove the ideas they already have about how males and females behave.

The effects of gender concepts and stereotypes

In the previous section, we have seen how children behave in different ways according to whether they perceive themselves to be boys or girls. There is a danger that children, who still hold strong gender stereotypes as adolescents

TRY THIS!

Read Chapter 1. Using the explanations of the various theories as to how children acquire behaviour, describe the ways in which children may acquire sex-role behaviour.

and young adults, will limit themselves to careers and activities that are traditionally 'male' or 'female'. There has been progress in the number of jobs and professions that are available for women that were traditionally for men only. There are now more women entering into medicine and the law than there are men. But some jobs are still predominately single sex, childcare being a prime example.

It has also been demonstrated that girls are more likely to choose non-traditional jobs if they consider themselves to be less feminine than other girls. These girls tend to have a higher self-esteem and feel confident in their abilities.

Within marriage and relationships, although more and more women continue to work outside of the home, they still do most of the domestic chores around the house. Sex-role concepts are powerful and slow to change.

What a strong girl you are!

Sex differences in children's behaviour

Experienced childcare practitioners recognise that boys and girls behave differently. Researchers have shown that these differences exist from infancy.

Girls respond more to people and social cues

- Girls establish and maintain eye contact more than boys. A difference that has been found in babies of one day old.
- Girl babies pay more attention to faces. By 6 months old, girls have a better memory for faces than boys and can tell the difference between two faces more easily than boys.

- From infancy (12 to 20 months), girls respond more if they hear another infant in distress than boys do.
- When mothers initiate social interactions with their babies by speaking to them, girls respond more readily than boys. This difference disappears if mothers initiate social interactions with their babies using a toy.

Boys respond more to physical cues

- Baby boys respond more to blinking lights, geometric patterns and objects than baby girls do.
- Baby boys have a better memory for the physical aspects of things, such as colour and shape than baby girls.

Rough and tumble play

- Several studies have shown that groups of boys engage in rough and tumble play between three and six times more frequently than girls, especially if they think that they are not being observed by adults. Rough and tumble play can consist of pretend fights which involve hitting, pushing and shoving.
- Boys are much more likely than girls to be involved in competitive team sports after school than girls.

Play parenting

- Girls engage in more play parenting games with dolls and domestic play things than boys.
- Girls are more likely than boys to respond to the needs of younger children.

Playing with toys

- Studies tend to show that boys play more with toys such as cars, mechanical objects and construction sets than do girls.
- Girls tend to spend more time mark making, drawing and painting than boys do and they play more with puzzles and materials such as clay.
- When drawing, boys are much more likely to draw technical things such as trucks, cars and aeroplanes than girls.

Fantasy play

- Girls' fantasy play tends to be associated with family themes such as looking after babies and domestic role play.
- Boys' fantasy play is more energetic and is associated with themes of power, dominance and conflict. It is common to see boys pretending to be characters they have seen on television.

These differences are partly to do with upbringing and societies expectations. However, three areas of research indicate that differences in children's behaviour may be influenced by biological factors.

- Cross-cultural studies tend to show similar differences in boys' and girls' behaviour.

- Studies of parents' treatment show that there is very little difference in the way that boys and girls are treated, at least in western cultures.
- Girls exposed to higher than normal levels of male sex hormone before they were born, tend to play in ways similar to the play of boys.

The differences in the ways that boys and girls behave worry some childcare practitioners. Girls seem to want to engage in activities that are valued by adults because they relate directly to the curriculum. Little boys, however, prefer to enter into noisy games outside. These views may be stereotypical, but, as we have seen, research has shown such differences. It is possible that negative attitudes from female childcare practitioners may be having an adverse effect on boys' development. Boys are doing less well in the educational system at all levels and they are more likely than girls to be excluded from school. We need to recognise that boys are often interested in different things from girls and we should use their enthusiasms as a starting point for developing a curriculum that meets their needs.

✔ PROGRESS CHECK

1 What is gender concept?

2 What three elements make up a child's gender concept?

3 In what ways can holding sex-role stereotypes limit a child's opportunities?

4 How can parents and childcare practitioners limit the negative effects of sex-role stereotyping?

5 How can childcare practitioners use the themes in boys' play to deliver the curriculum?

ETHNIC IDENTITY

Britain today is a multicultural, multi-ethnic society with citizens who can trace their origins from all over the world. In some schools, it is possible to find children who can trace their family back to the Norman Conquest or the arrival of the Huguenots. Some Jewish children may have ancestors who fled persecution in Europe. Other children have grandparents or parents who have come from the West Indies, the Indian subcontinent, Ireland or China. Britain's connections with countries all over the world have drawn people who have been eager to contribute to the nation's progress and have sought economic stability for their families. Many have seen Britain as a refuge from injustice and tyranny in their own countries and have come to Britain as asylum seekers or refugees. Thus it is that the children we care for can come from diverse ethnic backgrounds, and part of their self-concept will be their ethnic identity. However, before children can identify with an ethnic group they need to be have developed **ethnic awareness**.

DEFINITION

ethnic awareness the ability to recognise an individual's race or ethnic group

The development of ethnic awareness and identification

Francis Aboud (1988) undertook research into children in the USA and came to the following conclusions about the development of ethnic awareness and identification in children. She considers that before children can identify with a particular ethnic group, for instance being English, Indian or Chinese, they first need to become aware that different ethnic groups exist.

- Most children can point out people who are black or white at about 4 years old. This does not depend on their own ethnic background.

- Recognition of people whose ethnic backgrounds are Chinese or from the Indian subcontinent appears a few years later (for non-Chinese and non-Indian children) because the distinctions are not so easy for children to recognise.

- It is not until children are about 7 years of age that they can accurately categorise people into ethnic groups.

- By 8 years of age, children realise that an individual's ethnicity is stable and does not change.

- As children grow older, they pay less attention to the ethnic group to which the individual belongs and more to the specific characteristics of the person.

Once children begin to become aware of different ethnic groups they begin to be able to identify their own ethnic background.

- Most white children of 4 years of age can correctly point out a photograph of a child most like them from a selection of photographs of children of different ethnic backgrounds.

- Fewer black children can do this at the age of 4 years but, by the ages of 6 or 7 years, all children are able to do this.

- Asian children can usually all identify photographs of children like themselves by about 8 years of age.

The effects of racial prejudice

Unfortunately, **racial prejudice** exists in Britain today. Although, in the last thirty years there has been a growth of understanding and an increased sensitivity about such issues, negative attitudes towards those of different ethnic backgrounds still exist. You may encounter a variety of different terms used to describe racial prejudice such as racism and discrimination. In this text, the word '**prejudice**' is used to describe negative thoughts, feelings and behaviour towards a group of people. Groups who have been subject to prejudice include:

- religious groups, such as those from the Jewish and Roman Catholic faiths
- people with disabilities
- homosexuals
- women
- ethnic minorities.

Racial prejudice is prejudice specifically directed at people of a different ethnic group.

Self-esteem

As mentioned previously, our self-esteem is an evaluation of how close our self-image is to our ideal self. The closer our self-image is to our ideal self, the higher our self-esteem. Children who are subject to prejudice and negative attitudes may internalise these attitudes and develop feelings of low self-esteem.

Research into levels of self-esteem among children of different ethnic groups does not altogether support the view that children from ethnic minority groups have low self-esteem. Research undertaken among African American children in the USA did not find any difference in levels of self-esteem in these children compared to white children. However, children from other minority groups such as Hispanic children do appear to have lower levels of self-esteem.

Inequality

Negative attitudes towards children may also promote inequality of opportunity. Children from ethnic minorities may come from families who are at a disadvantage regarding housing, education, employment and access to health care. Previously, it was discussed that girls may not consider some forms of employment because the occupations are perceived to be 'male' jobs. In the same way, children from ethnic minorities may not consider certain forms of employment because there are no role models of people in these jobs who are from their ethnic group. In the same way, teachers may hold certain stereotypes about ethnic groups and this may affect the advice given to children about careers.

School exclusions

The number of children excluded from school has risen over the past few years with about 13,500 in 1996/7. Although this is a problem mainly of secondary schools, nearly 18 per cent of exclusions were from primary schools. The majority of excluded children are white boys, but statistics show that 16 per cent are from ethnic minorities, with nearly half of these being African-Caribbean children. Yet African-Caribbean children make up only 1 per cent of the school population (Social Exclusion Unit 1998).

A report from OFSTED in 1996 found that there was a high level of tension and conflict between white teachers and African-Caribbean pupils. Some teachers clearly held negative stereotypes about African-Caribbean children, they were highly critical and had low expectations of the children's abilities. In fact, African-Caribbean children who were excluded often had higher abilities than average, but were underachieving at school.

> **THINK ABOUT IT**
>
> Using the information found earlier in this chapter, draw up a list of characteristics that you could see in a child with low self-esteem.

▽ GOOD
PRACTICE

These points are particularly valuable if you have no children from different ethnic backgrounds in your establishment, as they will contribute to the development of the children's ethnic awareness.

- Have an equal opportunity/anti-bias policy, which is reviewed frequently.
- It is not acceptable for childcare practitioners to behave in a prejudicial way towards the children they care for. Establishments should implement good quality equal opportunities training.
- Do not allow staff, parents or visitors to use racist, or stereotypical language.
- Gently challenge prejudicial behaviour in other children. Explain, according to the children's age, why this behaviour is not liked.
- Raise children's feelings of self-worth by having resources, such as books, that show children and adults like themselves in active, positive roles.
- From time to time include stories, rhymes and music from different ethnic backgrounds.
- Have examples of writing from different languages visible around the room.
- Incorporate clothes and utensils from different ethnic groups in the home corner.

- Celebrate diversity by incorporating festivals from different religions into the establishment's programme.
- Show respect for all parents, regardless of ethnic group and give all of them a chance to help out from time to time.
- Discuss with parents any cultural/religious needs of the children. The establishment may need to consider translating material given to parents or using an interpreter.
- Parents, regardless of ethnic group, might enjoy sharing songs and stories from their childhood with the children or cooking a traditional meal.
- Expect high levels of achievement from all the children.
- In order to prevent exclusions of children who show inappropriate behaviour there should be an appropriate discipline/behaviour policy that is applied consistently. This subject is looked at in more detail in Chapter 4.
- As far as possible, the childcare team should reflect the ethnic background of the children. Selection and recruitment procedures should encourage applications from staff of all ethnic and cultural backgrounds.
- Staff from different ethnic backgrounds should be seen to be in positions of responsibility.

Discuss with parents any cultural or religious needs

KEY TERMS

You need to know the meaning of the following words and phrases. Go back through the chapter to make sure you understand them:

ethnic awareness
ethnic identity
gender identity
gender stability
ideal self
identification
prejudice
racial prejudice
self-esteem
self-image
sex-role behaviour
sex-role concept
sex-role stereotyping
self-concept

✔ PROGRESS CHECK

1 Define ethnic awareness and ethnic identity.
2 Outline the patterns of development of ethnic identity.
3 How can you promote feelings of self-worth for children from **all** ethnic backgrounds.

FURTHER READING

Aboud, F. (1988) *Children and Prejudice,* Blackwell
    Although published some time ago, this book contains the results of some interesting research of use to students on courses at Level 3 and above.
Blatchford, P. (1999) 'The state of play in schools', Chapter 5, in Woodhead, M., Faulkner, D. and Littlejohn, K. (eds) *Making Sense of Social Development*, Routledge in association with The Open University
    This chapter looks at rough and tumble play and is a useful text for students studying at Level 4.
Napier, J., 'Violent games', in *Nursery World*, page 10, 11 May 2000
    This is an excellent article on boys' participation in war games and superhero play. It will be useful for students on courses of all levels.
Rodd, J. (1996) *Understanding Young Children's Behaviour*, Allen and Unwin
    Chapter 3 is particularly useful.

Both these texts give good accounts of the development of the self-concept and will be useful for students on Level 3 courses.
Bee, H. (1995) *The Developing Child,* Longman
Gross, R. (1996) *Psychology, the Science of Mind and Behaviour*, Hodder and Stoughton

Managing behaviour in childcare settings

This chapter includes:

- The general principles of behaviour management
- Behaviour management in the family setting
- Behaviour management in nurseries, pre-schools and nursery classes
- Behaviour management in the infant school
- Child protection.

Childcare practitioners are in a unique position. They are in a position to be able to promote positive behaviour in children and are in a position to support children and their families if a child's behaviour is giving cause for concern. A whole team approach backed up by the use of effective policies and procedures is needed to help children learn appropriate ways of behaving in childcare and education settings. In addition, effective observation and assessment of children can often identify potential issues early. Appropriate intervention may prevent a minor concern developing into a significant behaviour problem. Early identification and assessment of children with more serious difficulties will mean that children and families receive help and support as early as possible.

THE GENERAL PRINCIPLES OF BEHAVIOUR MANAGEMENT

In Chapter 1, we looked at the various ways that theorists have tried to explain why children behave as they do. Each theoretical approach gives rise to suggestions as to how appropriate behaviour can be encouraged and inappropriate behaviour modified. Behaviourist theories have led to methods of modifying children's behaviour based on positive and negative reinforcement. Social learning theorists stress the importance of children being exposed to positive role models if their behaviour is to be changed. In practice, effective behaviour management will draw on techniques that are based on a variety of theoretical approaches, although methods based on behaviourist theories predominate. Refer to Chapter 1 of this book so that you have an understanding of the various theoretical approaches to understanding children's behaviour.

Principle one: most behaviour is learned

Although, later in the book we will look at conditions that are inherited, or are caused by an impairment of the brain, most behaviour in children is learned in the following ways.

● Children will copy the behaviour of adults who are special to them, such as parents, childcare practitioners and teachers. Children will also copy behaviour seen on the television, or from older children.

Children will copy the behaviour of adults who are special to them

● Children will repeat behaviour that is followed by something pleasant, (positive reinforcement). For most children love, praise and attention are positive reinforcers, together with rewards such as sweets and treats. Feelings of satisfaction, pride or happiness are examples of positive reinforcers that come from within children.

● Children will tend not to repeat a behaviour if it is followed by something unpleasant, or is not rewarded. Paying no attention to a child who is behaving inappropriately (when possible) tends to lessen the chance that the behaviour will be repeated.

TRY THIS!

Look at the following list of behaviours. For each one decide if there is an age when this behaviour is appropriate. At what age would you consider the behaviour to be inappropriate? If a child of one year tipped his bowl of food on the floor, that would be considered normal for his age, but if a four-year-old did the same thing, then the behaviour would be inappropriate.

- A child wets the bed.
- A child takes a sweet from another child.
- A child wants a toy that another child is playing with and pushes the other child to get it.
- A child has a temper tantrum because he wants a bar of chocolate in the supermarket.
- A child scribbles over a story book.

- Sometimes we may assume that something is unpleasant for a child, such as a 'telling off', when the child actually finds the attention to be rewarding.

Principle two: have realistic expectations about behaviour

It is essential that childcare practitioners have a thorough knowledge of child development so that they know what behaviour to expect from a child of a certain age. Behaviour that would be considered inappropriate for a four-year-old, such as frequent temper tantrums, may be normal behaviour for a two-year-old child.

From this exercise you have probably realised that all these behaviours would be considered 'normal' behaviour at certain ages. If children are disciplined for 'normal' behaviour we could be putting them under immense psychological pressure which might have an adverse effect on their later development. It is far better to try and avoid conflict situations by thinking ahead and reorganising the environment. When you feed a one-year-old child you would make sure that, if food did fall on the floor, the surface was easy to clean up. (Chapter 2 contains a description of the term 'discipline' as it is used in this book.)

You can expect a one-year-old child to make a mess at mealtimes

How children's behaviour changes with age

Table 4.1 on page 86 summarises the stages in development in children's behaviour from babyhood to school age. Childcare practitioners should have a detailed knowledge of how children behave at different ages and at the end of the chapter you will find recommendations for texts that will give more detailed information than can be given here.

Table 4.1　A brief summary of the stages in development in children's behaviour

Age	Normal behaviour	Behaviour management
Babies: under 1 year	Babies are too young to know what is acceptable behaviour and what is not. If they are hungry, cold or in pain they will cry to get your attention. They learn by exploring with their senses and have a tremendous drive to investigate anything they come across. According to how well they can control their muscles they will put things into their mouths, push, prod and investigate anything they can reach. If they see something they want they may grab it. They have no concept of 'mine' and 'not mine'.	Respond to babies' needs, provide security and comfort. Provide lots of opportunity for babies to explore in safety. Remove objects that will harm them. Make sure they cannot reach delicate or valuable items. 'Baby proof' the environment. Explain to older children that the baby is not being naughty and that they are too young to know any better. Provide a 'baby-free' environment so older children can play with their toys undisturbed. You could put the older child in a playpen with their constructional toys and leave the baby to crawl outside.
Toddlers: 1 to 3 years	Toddlers have a need to try and do things for themselves even though they haven't got the skills yet, such as dressing themselves. They can get very frustrated. They are unable to wait long before having their needs met and are prone to temper tantrums. They are unable to share with others or take turns. Toddlers are not very good at remembering what they have been told.	Be observant and distract them with something else if they are getting frustrated. Try to avoid situations where they might throw a temper tantrum. If you know that they will want sweets in the supermarket, give them a 'goody bag' of treats such as cheese sticks and raisins to distract them when you are shopping. Never let a temper tantrum make you change your mind. Decide on limits and stick to them.
Pre-school: 3 to 5 years	Children of this age are beginning to understand that other people have feelings and are beginning to understand 'mine' and 'not mine'. They want to be liked and are experimenting with language and the effect it has on others. They may use 'rude' words or sound disrespectful. They will still find turn taking and sharing a challenge.	Children are developing language skills so you can begin to explain about the feelings of others. Understand that their use of 'rude' words is an experiment, do not show an extreme reaction. Gently explain that you do not like the way they are speaking and give them more appropriate alternatives. Lots of positive reinforcement is needed to raise the child's self-esteem. Children will begin to understand 'rules'. Be consistent. Stick to limits.
Infant school age: 5 to 7 years	Children will use adults as role models and might copy their behaviour. Children might sound cheeky because they are trying to talk like a grown up. Children begin to avoid things they feel they are no good at. They may lose interest in reading and writing if these are difficult. May find concentration and focusing on school work a challenge.	Be a positive role model. Explain, gently, that the way they are talking is inappropriate. Raise self-esteem, give support and encouragement to try things that are difficult. Give extra attention if they are finding work difficult. Reorganise the environment to encourage better concentration. Children will understand rules and are able to listen to reason. Sometimes still finds sharing and turn taking difficult.

In addition to having realistic expectations about children's behaviour for their age, it is also important to take account of the cultural and family group that the child comes from. In some families, boys are not expected to do any domestic work and it would be inappropriate to discipline a boy if he refuses to help clear up after a meal time if this behaviour is a girl's job at home. The childcare practitioner should gently explain to the child that nursery is different from home and that, here, we all help each other.

Principle three: set limits to children's behaviour

Children feel safe and secure when there are boundaries and limits are set. It helps them know how far they can go, what is acceptable and what is not. Rules also help children predict how others will behave. Expectations about how the children are to behave should be realistic and appropriate for their age. All staff, parents and, of course, the children should be told clearly what these expectations are. All childcare establishments will have to work out their own expectations of what they want children to do and not to do, but most establishments would agree that behaviour is unacceptable if:

● it puts the child or others in danger
● it is hurtful or offensive to others
● it causes property to be damaged.

Behaviour policies will be discussed later in this chapter.

Principle four: be consistent

Research has shown that if discipline is applied inconsistently, the inappropriate behaviour may actually be strengthened. If a child asks for something and you say 'No' the child has to understand that if you say 'No' you mean 'No'. Children soon learn that if they keep on and on, some adults might change their mind. By being inconsistent you could be encouraging the children not to accept 'No' for an answer and that by crying or making a fuss they will get what they want.

If Mummy has said that you can't have a biscuit then you can't have a biscuit!

Being consistent also means that all the adults involved in the care of the child expect the same behaviour. Good team work and communication between the childcare team and with the child's parents are essential.

Principle five: try to understand why the child is behaving in an inappropriate way

To understand why children behave in a particular way, childcare practitioners need to gather information from a variety of sources:

Observing children will help you understand their behaviour

- from parents and carers who can tell you about the child's background and previous experiences. Childcare practitioners should be aware of any major influences in the child's life that could result in inappropriate behaviour, as well as day-to-day events such as staying up late that might make the child grumpy the next day
- from other professionals, such as the child's previous childcare practitioners or professionals involved in the child's care if they have a condition such as autism
- from observing the child himself.

When observing children's behaviour, the ABC model has been found to be useful. In this model, the child's key worker will undertake an event sample (see Table 4.2) to record instance of inappropriate behaviour over a period of time. The event sample records:

- **A**ntecedents – what was happening to the child immediately before the incident
- **B**ehaviour – what the child did that was inappropriate
- **C**onsequences – what happened as a result of the behaviour.

Table 4.2: An example of an event sample

Name of child:

Date of birth:

Reason for observing behaviour:

Relevant family factors (Culture/religion/social circumstances/recent stressful event):

Relevant factors about the child (recent illnesses, social skills, any special needs):

Date and time	Exact description of the child's behaviour (what the child did and said)	What was happening immediately before incident	Consequences of child's behaviour

The number of days that the event sample is carried out will depend on the frequency of the child's inappropriate behaviour. The aim is to gather enough information so that you can see exactly what triggers the child's behaviour and whether what happens afterwards may actually encourage the child to behave inappropriately again.

Once you begin to understand why a child is behaving in this way you can begin to think of ways to modify this behaviour.

Principle six: be exact about what behaviour you want to change

If you have been conscientious about monitoring the child's behaviour, you will be in a good situation to decide what behaviour needs to be changed. For this you need to be specific. Instead of saying that you want the child to behave nicely, be exact about what behaviour you want to see. Do not try to change a child's behaviour all at once, be realistic and work on one thing at a time. You may decide that you want the child to sit down during story time and not wander around. Explain to the child exactly what you want them to do and the reason why.

Principle seven: decide on the method you will use to encourage the behaviour change and involve everyone in the child's care as well as the child

For the majority of children, the most effective method is to use a positive approach. In this method, as far as possible, the inappropriate behaviour is ignored and, when the child behaves in the way you want, the child is praised and given positive attention. Older children may respond to being given a star for appropriate behaviour, with a reward at the end of the day if they have a certain number of stars.

Principle eight: never use physical punishment or humiliate a child

The use of physical punishment and its use by parents has been discussed in Chapter 2. The use of physical punishment in most childcare and education settings is illegal. Recently, however, the government has indicated that child-minders can 'smack' a child if the parents have given their express permission for this to happen. As was discussed in Chapter 2, there is still great debate in Britain about the use of physical punishment for children. Even some childcare practitioners, who would never hit a child in their workplace, would consider hitting their own child. There are several compelling reasons why children should not be subjected to physical punishment.

- There is a moral issue. Is it right for one individual to be violent towards another? If an adult hit another adult, he or she would be guilty of breaking the law. It is especially wrong if an adult hits a child. The adult is physically bigger than the child and is in a position of power and

Discuss your worries with the parents

other factors operating of which you are unaware. Good communication involves listening and being open to suggestions.

Some nannies may feel apprehensive about talking to parents about discipline. It is easier to raise the topic if, at interview, or on the first day, you bring up the subject of 'house rules'. You may mention then that you will tell them how things are going once you have settled in. If the parents and you decide that there needs to be a change in how you expect the children to behave, then you and the parents together should discuss this with the children so there is no misunderstanding and the children can see that there is agreement between all the adults.

Appropriate 'house rules'

It is not possible to write a set of rules that will be appropriate for all situations. What is included will depend on many factors such as:

- whether you are a nanny in the children's home or you are a childminder looking after children in your home
- the numbers of children
- the ages and abilities of the children
- the wishes of the parents
- the layout and equipment in the house
- the time of day that you look after the children
- any activities undertaken outside the home. Do you take the children in your car, do they ride bikes on the pavement, do they play outside?

Whatever the circumstances, the rules should be phrased positively, emphasising the behaviour you expect to see, rather than a set of 'Do nots'. For example you expect children to behave in a way that:

- is safe to themselves and others
- is kind to others
- respects the property of others.

A positive approach to managing children's behaviour

Young children respond well to a positive approach to managing their behaviour that aims to avoid conflict situations and encourages appropriate behaviour. A positive approach involves the following.

- Altering the environment so that the children can play safely rather than having to be told not to touch things or to stay away from dangerous equipment. This would include the use of safety items such as fire guards, stair gates and cooker guards.

- Having a good knowledge of child development so that you do not have unrealistic expectations, such as expecting a toddler to share.

- Using your knowledge of the child to avoid conflict situations, such as recognising when a child is getting tired and frustrated and telling them to have a nap, or remembering to take their comforter with them on trips.

- Giving children plenty of time to clear up or get ready for school. Some childcare practitioners have found that gradually dimming lights helps children realise that time is passing. Others have used big egg timers or a special piece of music that gives children time to get ready.

- If you want children to behave in a certain way, praise them and give them lots of attention for any attempt to behave in the way you want. They will be more likely to repeat the desired behaviour again. If children see you giving attention to other children who are behaving well, they are more likely to copy the behaviour.

- Ignore unwanted behaviour as far as possible. Sometimes even negative attention can be rewarding for a child.

- Try not to be negative. Instead of telling children what not to do, think of a way of making the statement more positive. Instead of saying, 'Do not scribble on the wall', you could give the child some paper and say 'We do our drawing on this paper'. When the child starts drawing on the paper you need to praise them and give them attention.

- Always give an explanation why you expect children to behave in a certain way.

- Be a good role model yourself. You cannot expect children to learn appropriate behaviour if you use bad language, are rude, impolite and aggressive.

- Do not step in too quickly when children are having an argument. Learning how to handle conflict situations is important and children need to experiment and find out how their behaviour affects others. You should monitor the situation closely and be ready to step in if things are getting out of hand. When the children have calmed down, talk to them about what happened and ask them if they could have handled the situation better. Suggest alternative ways of behaving the next time.

✔ PROGRESS CHECK

1 What are the main differences between looking after your own children and looking after other people's children in a family situation?

2 How would you go about establishing a set of 'house rules' if you were a nanny in a family home and how might this differ if you were a child-minder?

3 Describe the positive approach to managing children's behaviour.

4 How would you deal with the following situations:

- a child having a temper tantrum in the supermarket

- a four-year-old pulling away from your hand in the street and running into the road

- a five-year-old telling you that you are a 'silly old cow'

- an eighteen-month-old pushing another child because he wants a toy?

BEHAVIOUR MANAGEMENT IN NURSERIES, PRE-SCHOOLS AND NURSERY CLASSES

In the previous section, we looked at ways of managing children's behaviour in the family situation. Many of the suggestions made are still appropriate for the nursery situation, but there are differences. These include:

- childcare practitioners work in a team often consisting of trained and untrained staff

- most nurseries have a hierarchical system of management with a nursery manager, co-ordinator or teacher who has overall responsibility

- nurseries have policies and set procedures which guide practice

- where large groups of children are being looked after together, issues of safety and the way children interact together become increasingly important.

A behaviour management policy

It is important that everyone involved in the nursery is working together to manage children's behaviour. An effective behaviour policy will facilitate good team work.

Drawing up the policy

It is not possible to write a behaviour policy that will be appropriate for all childcare establishments because so many different factors have to be taken into account. New managers may be tempted to use a policy that has been drawn up by another nursery, but even if the two establishments are similar it is always best for a staff team to write their own policy because this leads to deeper understanding and an increased commitment to make things work.

If a staff team writes its own behaviour policy it will lead to an increased commitment to make things work

When drawing up a behaviour policy there are several considerations.

1   Some thought needs to be given to who is going to draw up the behaviour policy. In an ideal situation, the policy should be drawn up in consultation with staff (including administrative and domestic staff), parents and other people who are connected with the establishment such as steering groups or management committees. Older children will also be able to contribute their ideas, if care is taken to present the subject at a level that they understand. If people are involved with the production of policies, they will feel a sense of ownership and will be in a good position to put policy into practice. Some staff, especially those who are untrained or inexperienced may feel that they do not have the necessary skills to be involved. In this situation, appropriate in-service training should be arranged. Managers could provide this training themselves, or make use of existing courses run by others, such as the local authority.

2   Draw up a code of behaviour for the children. This will need to be clear and simple for the under-fives. Suitable items to include would be:

● be kind
● be careful
● be safe
● you must not hurt anybody.

In addition, staff need to decide on more explicit rules such as:

● only four children in the home corner at one time
● no running inside
● no name calling.

These rules should be kept to a minimum and must be clearly communicated to all staff, the parents and the children. Too many rules will be confusing and very young children will not remember them.

3 Decide what methods you will use to modify children's behaviour. All staff need to know that physical punishment and humiliation are not to be used. In nurseries, as in family situations, positive methods are the most effective way of managing children's behaviour.

4 Decide if there is sufficient detail in the policy for it to be used as a guide to good practice, or whether you need to go into more detail in some sections and draw up specific procedures. You may want to write a detailed procedure document outlining the methods you will use in the nursery to modify children's behaviour, leaving the policy with a brief statement that positive methods will be used.

5 Decide how you will let everyone know about the policy. Staff need to be informed at the next staff meeting, noting any staff who are absent so that they can be told later. Parents could be informed via letter home and perhaps an evening meeting. The policy should also be included in the information booklet that parents are given when their child starts nursery, and should be one of the topics that are discussed with parents before they accept a place for their child.

Implementing the policy

- Rules must be applied consistently by everyone including staff members such as administrative and domestic staff. Students need to be introduced to the behaviour policy as part of their induction process.

- Parents need to uphold the rules while their children are still on the premises. Parents should challenge their children if they see them 'breaking' a nursery rule such as running in the classroom.

Evaluating and reviewing the policy

Policies need to be evaluated from time to time. That means that staff need to discuss whether the policy is effective. It is difficult to be **objective** about whether or not the policy is working. You may be able to look at evidence such as an incident book or the daily diary to see if there are fewer problems with behaviour reported. Staff can be asked for their impressions, or asked to rate on a scale of one to ten how effective they think the policy has been. Methods that rely on asking staff their opinions are more **subjective** and may not be so reliable.

The value of routine

As well as an effective behaviour policy, nurseries can help children manage their own behaviour by establishing an effective routine to the day. Children feel secure when they can predict what is about to happen, as they know what they are supposed to be doing and gain comfort in being able to predict what others are about to do. Routines need to have an element of flexibility so that staff can react to unexpected events, such as a fall of snow and children should have a degree of choice about what they are going to do. Each session or day should have a predictable framework which encourages choice and flexibility with in it. In an established nursery, 'new' children will quickly

---

▽ **GOOD PRACTICE**

Policies also need to be reviewed from time to time to ensure that the policy is still relevant. There may have been a new piece of outside equipment introduced into the nursery and it is obvious that there needs to be an additional safety rule added.

DEFINITIONS

objective   a judgment based on independent evidence, not influenced by personal feelings or opinions

subjective   a judgment influenced by personal opinions and feelings

There are various ways of getting the attention of young children, if they are deeply involved in activities, such as:

- ringing a bell or triangle
- using a non-verbal signal such as the childcare practitioner putting her hand on her head. Children know when they see the signal they need to be quiet. Gradually the noise level will quieten and all the children will be attending.

get the hang of the routine by following what the other children are doing, especially if their key worker makes sure that they know what is happening. It is important that childcare practitioners are sensitive to the need to give young children plenty of time for transitions. If you suddenly tell children that it is tidy up time, some children may pay no attention because they are deeply involved in an activity. Techniques to manage transitions have been discussed previously and involve methods such as dimming the lights, using a bell as a five minute warning and using a giant sand timer.

Arranging the environment

As in the family setting, you can encourage children to behave appropriately by arranging the environment thoughtfully.

- Children need a safe environment so that they are not always being told not to do things.

- Free access to a large enough outside play area should be provided. Much inappropriate behaviour in children could just be the result of children being confined too long in a small space. Most childcare practitioners are aware of the change in children's behaviour when they have been unable to play outside because of the weather.

- Wide open spaces within the nursery classrooms are an invitation for children to run. Arrange the furniture so that children do not see all the space at once.

- Arrange the environment so that every area can be monitored by staff. With imagination, it is possible to use furniture and dividers to direct 'traffic flow'. You can divide the space into different activity areas, or

Children need access to an outside play area

CASE STUDY

Joshua is 4 years old and attends a private day nursery full time. Joshua has a long day. The nursery is attached to his mother's workplace and they have an hour-long car ride to get to nursery in the morning, when he is dropped off at 8.30. In the evening he is picked up at 5.30 for the hour-long drive back home. It is often not until 9 o'clock that Joshua goes to bed because his parents have to make the evening meal, bath him and read him a story. Joshua is often irritable in nursery, and the staff find that he sometimes needs a sleep in the morning. The main concern for Joshua's key worker is Joshua's poor concentration skills and inability to sit still for very long. He flits from activity to activity, rarely focusing on anything for more than a minute or two. During story time, Joshua will shout out and is unable to wait until he is asked for his comments. Joshua has a short temper and cannot wait to have any of his needs met. He finds it difficult to share and the other children avoid playing with him because he will push them if he wants a toy that they are playing with.

1 How might Joshua's poor concentration skills adversely affect his education?

2 Joshua's key worker is concerned and thinks that he should be put on the establishment's register of children with special educational needs. Describe what action she should take.

3 What are the establishment's responsibilities towards Joshua's parents?

4 What methods could be used to try and find out the extent of Joshua's difficulties?

5 What action could be taken, initially, to help Joshua?

6 After reviewing this initial action, it is decided to move Joshua onto stage two of the identification and assessment procedure. Suggest a suitable action plan for him.

BEHAVIOUR MANAGEMENT IN INFANT SCHOOLS

Managing the behaviour of children in infant school can be more of a challenge than managing the behaviour of children in the nursery situation. The main reasons for this are:

- The adult:child ratio is higher. Although efforts are being made to reduce the numbers of children in infant classrooms, there are still more children per adult than in a nursery.

- Children are expected to be more independent than they were in nursery. The environment is larger and children will be expected to move sensibly from the classroom to the hall, playground and dining areas which all may be some distance from one another.

- The day is more structured. There are more whole class activities where children need to be quiet to listen to the teacher. The literacy and numeracy initiatives have made it increasingly important that children are able to concentrate and work independently. Children will be given tasks to complete on their own, while the teacher and classroom assistant are busy with other children.

- The play areas are bigger, with more children using them. 'Play time' at mid-morning break can be a challenge for some children.
- Infant classes may contain children who are only just 4 years old. Children of this age frequently need an afternoon nap and may behave in ways that adults consider to be inappropriate because they are too young and too tired to cope with the demands that are put upon them.

The children in an infant class have all arrived with different experiences of pre-school care and education, ranging from children who have been in nursery since they were babies, to children who have had no pre-school educational experience at all. Children also vary in their home circumstances. Generally speaking, children from stable home environments, where limits have been set on their behaviour, adjust to the behavioural expectations of infant class better than children from less stable backgrounds. It would be wrong to assume that all children from disrupted backgrounds will have behaviour difficulties. Such a stereotypical view is not helpful:

- it can lead to a self-fulfilling prophesy about the way a child could behave
- it can lead to very poor home/school links
- it can make staff feel that nothing they can do will change the influence of home background.

The school's behaviour policy

TRY THIS!

Gather examples of behaviour policies from local schools. Compare the policies to see what they have in common and if there are any differences. If you are doing this as a member of a group in college you could compare all the policies that the other students have collected.

Schools will have a behaviour policy that outlines the expectations the school has for the way that children will behave. Occasionally a child may need to be excluded. School policies will need to have clear criteria for exclusion and a plan for the re-integration of the child.

Bullying

As part of their behaviour policy, or as a separate policy, most schools have developed procedures to deal with any incidents of bullying that occur within the school. Many children have had their education blighted because they were bullied at school. Occasionally, children have become so desperate that they have taken their own lives. In less extreme situations children have refused to attend school, or continue to attend school but are unable to make the most of their education because of the emotional distress they are under. The children who are bullies may also be victims of circumstances that have lead them to express their emotional disturbance by hurting other children.

A policy that addresses bullying in schools should contain procedures to be followed if an incident of bullying is suspected, together with advice for all children on ways to protect themselves.

Anti-bullying guidelines for schools

- The whole school should be involved in anti-bullying initiatives, i.e. pupils, parents, teachers, ancillary staff and head teacher and governors.

- Have a set of procedures for dealing with incidents. Make it clear to staff and children that bullying (by children or adults) will not be tolerated.
- Adequate supervision of all outside play areas will reduce the incidence of bullying.
- Encourage anyone who is being bullied or has witnessed bullying to tell somebody.
- Think of easy ways for children to tell adults what is happening. One suggestion is to have 'bully boxes' where children can leave notes about incidents.
- Hold assemblies about bullying.
- Teachers need to discuss bullying with their classes. Not just once, but regularly.
- In schools where children are old enough, set up a system of peer counselling where younger children can seek advice from older children who have been trained and are being supported in their role.
- Put up anti-bullying posters.
- Have a selection of resources that children and teachers can use.

Advice for children if they are being bullied

Teachers, parents and childcare professionals need to help children who are being bullied by giving them specific strategies to try out. The following advice may be helpful.

- Bullies often pick on someone because they know the 'victim' will cry or behave in a way that the bully finds 'funny'. Children who are bullied should be advised to ignore the bully and walk away if they can and try not to cry or get angry. They should not try to fight back because that makes it worse. Instead they should shout 'No' very loudly. Role play is an effective way of practising this in a 'safe' situation.

No! I don't like it

- Suggest funny or clever remarks that the child can use. It sometimes puts a bully off, especially if the bully loses face in front of his friends.
- If a bully has said something unpleasant, suggest that the child asks the bully to repeat the remark again. Saying the same thing twice often makes the comment seem ridiculous, even to the bully.
- Suggest that the child who is being bullied avoids being alone and avoids situations where there are no adults around. This will protect them.
- Above all, request that the child tell a friend or another adult what is happening.

✔ PROGRESS CHECK

1 Why do some children find it difficult to behave appropriately in infant school when they had no behaviour difficulties in nursery?

2 Staff sometimes assume that children from certain backgrounds will have more difficulties than others in behaving appropriately in school. What may be the negative effect of such assumptions?

3 What can schools do to protect the children from bullying?

4 What advice can you give to a child who is being bullied?

CHILD PROTECTION

Several of the topics looked at already in this chapter, such as the use of physical punishment and bullying, are child protection issues. Childcare practitioners should be able to recognise the signs that a child is being abused, know what to do with their suspicions and know how to protect themselves from allegations of abuse.

THINK ABOUT IT

Why are children with behaviour difficulties more at risk of physical abuse than other children?

Children who have challenging behaviour may be more at risk of being physically abused because adults find this behaviour difficult to cope with. It is easy to see that adults might lose their temper when dealing with such children. Some parents lose control and may beat their children severely. Occasionally, a childcare practitioner is reported in the news as having hit a child in her care. In other situations parents may truly believe that harsh physical punishment will correct their children's behaviour. You may have heard of the phrase 'Spare the rod and spoil the child'. Parents might feel that they have a biblical justification in beating their children, although one interpretation of the phrase is that the 'rod' is the word of God and has nothing to do with physical punishment at all.

Behavioural symptoms of child abuse

For some children, behavioural difficulties may actually be the symptom of abuse rather than the cause of it. Any form of abuse whether it be physical, sexual or neglect will also involve emotional abuse. A child who is emotionally abused will have low self-esteem and may have very negative feelings about themselves.

TRY THIS!

In a small group discuss how being abused could have a negative effect on a child's behaviour.

Children who have been abused may show some of the following behaviour:

- withdrawal, tearfulness or depression
- regression, reverting back to an earlier stage of behaviour. This can involve demanding to be spoon fed, wanting a dummy or having to go back into nappies
- not being interested in play
- aggression towards other children
- lack of concentration/drop in standard of school work
- not wanting to try new things for fear of failure
- defiance
- disorders of appetite (eating more or less than usual)
- changes in sleep pattern
- sexualised behaviour/play.

Child protection policy and procedures

Child protection establishments are required to have a child protection policy. This should conform to the local authority's procedures which will specify the role of staff in the various different types of facilities that care for young children. It is important that all staff receive training in child protection and that everyone is aware of an establishment's policy and procedures.

The policy should include:

- measures to protect children from adults working in the establishment (police checks, taking up references, interviewing, supervision, procedures that outline how staff are to undertake intimate care and so on)
- behaviour management guidelines
- anti-bullying guidelines
- procedures to follow if abuse is suspected.

Dealing with suspicions of child abuse

At some time in their careers most child care practitioners will suspect that a child in their care is being abused, either by someone connected to the child outside of the childcare and education facility (such as a parent) or by someone within the establishment. Often suspicions are alerted by changes in a child's behaviour or by bruises or other marks on a child's body. Sometimes a child will tell you what has happened. It is essential that you pass on suspicions to the relevant authorities because there may already be concerns about the welfare of the child. Your information could be all that is needed for the authorities to take action to protect the child. If you suspect a child is being abused:

- follow your establishment's procedures
- discuss your worries with your line manager (if you have one)
- make a written record of your concerns. If you are recording details of physical signs such as bruises, use a diagram to record the position of the

mark. Sign and date your record and ask your line manager to read it and sign it as well. Records must be written within 24 hours of the incident.

- be careful about questioning the child about what has happened. You can ask general questions such as, 'That bruise looks painful, what happened?', but not direct questions such as 'Did Daddy get angry and hit you again?' If you ask 'leading' questions you might be accused of putting words into the child's mouth

- if you are decide to inform social services and it is one of the child's parents whom you suspect, gently tell the parent of your worries and what you intend to do. The only exception to this is if you suspect a parent of sexually abusing the child because the parent may frighten the child into not telling anyone what has happened

- when telephoning the social services department make sure you have the child's personal details with you. You will be asked to give details such as the child's name, address and date of birth.

Dealing with child protection issues is always stressful. You may find you remember painful incidents in your own childhood, or you may worry about what a parent will say if you have had to inform social services about them. You could be feeling very upset for the child and angry about what has happened to him or her. It always helps to discuss these worries with others (maintaining confidentiality of course) Many establishments have a system of regular supervision sessions for childcare practitioners and these sessions can help you deal with some of these issues. Your GP can also refer you for counselling if you are being affected by incidents that happened to you as a child.

Supporting the child

- If a child tells you that she is being abused, try to remain calm and supportive. If you show too much emotion the child may be too frightened to say anything else.

- Let the child know that you believe what she is saying and that she is not to blame for what happened to her.

- Do not make any promises to the child. She may want you to promise not to tell anyone, but you will have to gently tell her that you may have to involve others.

- Listen to what the child is saying but don't ask questions. As soon as possible, make a written record of what the child has said.

- Children who are being abused may be under considerable stress. Chapter 7 contains information on helping stressed children.

Protecting yourself from allegations of abuse

Sometimes children are harmed by staff entrusted with their care. Staff may be temperamentally unsuited to work with children. They may lose their temper easily and may be verbally or physically aggressive. There are a few individuals who get pleasure in physically or sexually abusing children and they may seek employment in childcare. With good selection and recruitment procedures, the risk of employing such individuals is reduced. However,

KEY TERMS

You need to know the meaning of the following words and phrases. Go back through the chapter and make sure you understand them:

Individual Education Plan
objective
Statement of Special Educational Need
statutory assessment
subjective

childcare and education practitioners need to be vigilant and not assume that a colleague would never harm a child. In the same way, childcare practitioners need to protect themselves from allegations of abuse. Measures include:

- avoiding being alone with children
- if you are involved in intimate care such as nappy changing or toileting, make sure other staff members know where you are and what you are doing. Keep doors open and try and ensure you can be seen by other staff members. If children need their underclothes changing because of an 'accident', encourage the children to wash and put on clean pants themselves if they are old enough
- always take another adult with you if you take a child out of the nursery, for instance for a walk in the park. Never give a child a lift in your car unless there is another staff member with you
- avoid having 'favourite' children
- some students worry about how much physical contact to give children. This all depends on the age of the child and should be according to the needs of the child rather than the needs of the adult. For instance, it is quite appropriate to give a three-year-old a cuddle if she is upset, but it is not appropriate to carry the child around and have them forever on your knee.

✔ PROGRESS CHECK

1 Why might children with behavioural difficulties be more at risk of child abuse than other children?

2 What behavioural changes might you see in a child who is being abused?

3 If a child aged 3 years came to the nursery with a red mark on her thigh that looks like the mark of a hand, what actions would you take?

4 How can childcare practitioners protect themselves from allegations of abuse?

FURTHER READING

There is a variety of books about bullying produced by Kidscape (contact information can be found in the section on Resources). The following is a selection.

DfEE (1994) *The Code of Practice for the Identification and Assessment of Children with Special Educational Needs*
This is essential reading for all those who are caring for children whose behaviour may adversely affect their progress in nursery/school.

Elliott, M. (1997) *101 Ways to Deal with Bullying: A Guide for Parents*, Kidscape
This book includes common-sense ideas to overcome problems, build self-esteem and make friends.

Elliott, M. *How to Stop Bullying*, Kidscape.
> This book has 90 practical anti-bullying exercises to use with students aged 5 to 16 and includes staff training and anti-bullying policies.

Hobart, C. and Frankel, J. (1998) *Good Practice in Child Protection*, Stanley Thornes
> This book gives practical information on child protection and is suitable for all students and practitioners.

Rodd, J. (1996) *Understanding Young Children's Behaviour*, Allen and Unwin
> This book gives an excellent account of the principles and practice of managing children's behaviour in early years settings. It will be useful for students on Level 3 and Level 4 courses.

Roffey, S. and O'Reirdan, T. (1997) *Infant Classroom Behaviour, Needs, Perspectives and Strategies*, David Fulton Publishers
> This book is full of very sensible, practical advice for all those managing children's behaviour in infant school. The book is clearly written and will be useful for students on childcare courses at all levels.

Under Fives Programme, Kidscape
> This is a manual for teaching young children about bullies, strangers, what to do if lost and saying 'No'.

Watkins, C. (2000) *Managing Classroom Behaviour*, Association of Teachers and Lecturers
> Chris Watkins, from the Institute of Education, is a national expert on behaviour management in schools. The guide is free for members of ATL, but can be purchased by non-members for £4.99. ATL Tel: no. 020 7930 6441.

These are useful books for finding information about age-appropriate behaviour.

Bruce, T. and Meggitt, C. (1999) *Child Care and Education*, Hodder and Stoughton

Sheridan, M. (1988) *From Birth to Five Years: Children's Developmental Progress*, NFER–Nelson

The professionals and therapies involved in managing children's behaviour

PREVIEW

This chapter includes:

- Professionals who may be involved in managing children's behaviour
- Therapies used in managing children's behaviour
- The work of family centres.

Most children will behave in ways that worry parents or childcare practitioners at some time in their lives but the majority of children will mature out of their difficulties with support from the adults who care for them. Some children will need more expert help, and in this chapter we will be looking at the professionals who may be involved in their assessment, treatment and long-term care. Throughout this book, various therapies are described. In this chapter, we will be looking, in more detail, at some of the most common ways of helping children. Many of these therapies are based on the theoretical approaches described in Chapter 1.

PROFESSIONALS WHO MAY BE INVOLVED IN MANAGING CHILDREN'S BEHAVIOUR

Parents or childcare practitioners may seek the help of experts at any time in a child's life. For babies and children not yet in the school system it is often a member of the primary health care team whose advice is sought, or who may be the first person to recognise that the child is experiencing difficulties.

When a child is at school it may be that the Special Educational Needs Co-ordinator (SENCO) seeks the advice of an educational psychologist. Sometimes the first professional who is consulted will refer the child to another professional and it is not unusual for children to see several people, all experts in different aspects of their care.

The primary health care team

Primary health care teams are based in the community and consist of:

- general practitioners
- health visitors
- community midwives
- community nurses.

These professionals either all work together based in a health centre, or may be based separately in GP surgeries and child health clinics. The members of the **primary health care** team who are most likely to be consulted first of all if parents are worried about an aspect of their child's behaviour are the general practitioner and the health visitor.

The primary health care team is responsible for treating illness in the community, preventing illness through health education, immunisation programmes and undertaking **screening** and **surveillance** programmes within the community. In stable communities, where there is not much movement of families or health professionals in and out of the area, families can build up good relationships with the various members of the primary health care team. In such situations parents feel more able to ask advice. Heath care professionals can use their knowledge of the family's circumstances and the facilities available in the community to provide the most appropriate care. In areas such as the middle of large cities, there is more movement of both families and health professionals and it is more difficult to build up stable relationships between families and primary health care teams.

General practitioners (GPs)

GPs (family doctors) are doctors who have undertaken a special training programme in general practice. Some GPs have an additional training in obstetrics, the care of women during pregnancy and labour, and are called GPOs. All of us should be registered with a GP who is then responsible for our medical care. GPs can work on their own or together with other GPs. Sometimes they may work from health centres where there are other health professionals such as practice nurses, community nurses, community midwives and health visitors. When we feel unwell, it is the GP who sees us. More often than not the GP is the only doctor we need to see, but sometimes the GP will refer us to hospital to see a doctor there if more specialist treatment is needed. If a parent has concerns about a child's health or behaviour, the GP is often the first professional to consulted. GPs are also involved in child health surveillance programmes. If another health professional such as a health visitor has concerns about a child's health or development the child will be referred to her GP.

Health visitors

Health visitors are Registered General Nurses who have undergone further training in health visiting. In addition, health visitors will be qualified midwives or have had training in obstetrics. Health visitors are key members of primary health care teams and have a vital role to play in promoting health in the community in which they work. Most health visitors work mainly with children and families, although they can contribute to the health care of people of all ages.

Health visitors can be based in GPs' surgeries and health centres where they look after everyone registered with the practice, or they can be based in clinics where they are responsible for a geographical area.

Health visitors are involved in the child health surveillance programme and all babies and children will be seen regularly until they reach school age, when the school nurse takes over. Health visitors visit families in their homes and will also see children in clinics where they are based. Often it is the health visitor to whom parents turn if they are concerned about aspects of their children's behaviour. Health visitors have expert knowledge in all aspects of caring for babies and children and will give advice and support to families facing difficult situations. Sometimes the health visitor may be the first person to recognise that a child is not well or is not developing as would be expected and the child will be referred to his GP. Health visitors work closely with other professionals involved in the health service, social services and educational services.

The school health service

Once children enter school, the school health service takes over the responsibility for routine child health surveillance. Children will continue to have

Often it is the health visitor to whom parents turn if they are worried about their children's behaviour

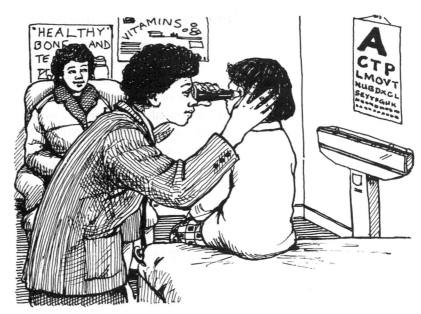

If children are not developing as expected, the paediatrician is asked to see them

regular check-ups throughout their school career when they will be seen by school doctors and school nurses. As part of their regular check-ups, children's hearing and vision will be tested and they will receive dental checks. The programme of immunisations started as babies will be continued throughout children's years at school.

School nurses

School nurses are Registered General Nurses or paediatric nurses who have taken additional training. School nurses are generally responsible for several schools in their area including primary schools, secondary schools and special schools. As well as being involved in the child health surveillance programme and the programme of immunisations, school nurses have an important role in health promotion, both for children and their parents. Parents are invited to attend their children's check ups and will often discuss behavioural difficulties with the school nurse who is in a good position to give help and advice.

Paediatrician

Paediatricians are medical doctors who have undertaken further training in paediatrics, the specialist care of children who are unwell. Most paediatricians work in hospitals and if GPs have concerns that children are not developing as expected, the paediatrician is asked to see them.

Psychiatrist

Psychiatrists are medical doctors who have taken further training in psychiatry, the care of individuals who have a mental illness. Some psychiatrists specialise in treating children and are called child psychiatrists.

Sometimes children have an overwhelming fear of dogs

dog on a lead would be a neutral stimulus since other people would not be afraid in this situation.

In **systematic desensitisation**, the aim of the treatment is to replace the fear reaction with a state of being relaxed. The following is a general outline of how a child may be treated.

- The therapist and the child agree the ultimate aim of the therapy sessions. It may be that the child should be able to walk to school, feeling relaxed, even if he meets a dog off a lead on the same side of the road as the child.

- The therapist talks to the child and finds out exactly in what circumstances the child begins to feel uneasy. The child may feel quite comfortable with a cartoon picture of a dog, but not with a fluffy toy dog or a photograph of a real dog.

- The child is taught relaxation techniques.

- The child is presented with a situation that makes him slightly uneasy. A fluffy toy dog may be put in front of him. The child is encouraged to use the relaxation techniques he has learned and the feelings of unease are replaced with feelings of relaxation.

- Once the child consistently feels relaxed when he sees the fluffy dog and can hold it and play with it quite happily, he is introduced to a slightly more fearful situation. This could be looking at a photograph of a real, fluffy dog. At the same time he is encouraged to use the relaxation techniques he has been taught.

- Gradually, over a series of sessions, the child is exposed to more and more potentially fearful situations, until he can be in the same room as a dog and walk to school quite happily.

Behaviour modification

Behaviour modification is based on the principles of operant conditioning, which is that any behaviour that is rewarded will tend to be repeated, any behaviour that is not rewarded, or produces an unpleasant result will tend not to be repeated. Behaviour modification is the most common method used for helping children towards more appropriate behaviour and the positive approaches to behaviour mentioned in the previous chapter are based on these principles. Whereas behaviour therapy is usually undertaken by trained therapists, behaviour modification can be used by parents and childcare professionals, sometimes following programmes designed by experts such as educational psychologists.

There is a wide variety of behaviour modification programmes, but generally they follow a similar pattern.

THINK ABOUT IT

What would be a good method to use to check the frequency of a child shouting out inappropriately in class?

- There needs to be a period of observation and assessment so that the behaviour that needs to be modified can be identified. It may be that a child is very noisy, frequently shouting out in class, or a child may not settle down to sleep at night without a tremendous fuss. It is useful if some measure of how frequently the child behaves inappropriately is taken so that a comparison can be made during the treatment programme to see if the programme is effective.

- We need to try to identify exactly what it is that is encouraging the child to behave inappropriately. Earlier on in the book, we have discussed how some children find being 'told off' rewarding because it gives them the attention that they crave. Children who make a fuss at night time may be being rewarded by being allowed to stay up later.

- The behaviour that we want to encourage needs to be identified. It may be that we want the child to raise their hand and wait to be asked before they talk in class, or we want the child to go to bed with no fuss and stay quietly in his bedroom.

- We need to find out what will be an appropriate reward for the child. Older children can be involved in discussions. It may be appropriate to give them a gold star for each night they go to bed with no fuss. These stars can be exchanged for a treat or a toy when they have 'earned' enough. Some children respond to praise and encouragement. Children who are showing attention-seeking behaviour may respond well if every time they show desirable behaviour they are rewarded with praise and attention. Their bad behaviour is ignored (as far as possible).

- All the adults involved in the care of the child must carry out the behaviour modification programme consistently. If the child is sometimes, unwittingly, rewarded for inappropriate behaviour, that behaviour will be strengthened.

- The length of time that the programme will be carried out has to be set and the child observed at regular intervals to see if the programme is being effective.

copying their behaviour from others. Behaviour is more likely to be copied if it is seen to be rewarded or if the person the child watches is someone they like, respect or has authority over them. Older children tend to copy the behaviour of their peers.

This has been used as a way to treat children who have phobias. In a series of experiments by Bandura in the 1970s, children who were afraid of dogs were shown films of other children playing with a variety of dogs. Children who watched these films were shown to be less afraid of dogs afterwards compared to children who just watched neutral films. Bandura went on to show that modelling was even more effective if phobic children were able to watch real children and dogs rather than a film. In nursery situations, children are more likely to behave appropriately if they see other children being praised for behaving well.

Cognitive behaviour therapy

There is a wide variety of approaches that concentrate on changing the way individuals think, as well as the way they behave.

Cognitive behaviour therapy can be used with older children who can express their thoughts and feelings. If an older child is afraid of dogs, as well as designing a behaviour modification programme, the therapist will ask them what they think about when confronted with a dog off a lead. The child might report a variety of negative thoughts such as, 'I'm nervous, I think the dog will bite me', 'I'm going to panic, I can't cope' or 'This is too hard, I can't do it'. The therapist will teach the child to replace negative, self-defeating thoughts with positive self-instructions such as, 'Be calm, I can cope, the dog is not interested in me'.

Children who are very frightened about exams can be helped by a combination of behavioural and cognitive techniques. Behavioural techniques may include organising revision into bite-size bits, rewarding themselves after revision sessions, plenty of practice in the exam situation so that their nervous system ceases to react (flooding) and learning how to relax. Cognitive techniques could include teaching children to say, to themselves, such as, 'I can do this exam, I have revised well, I know the subject back to front, I'm looking forward to demonstrating what I know.'

Psychoanalysis

In the same way that learning theory has given rise to ways of helping individuals based on this approach, Freudian theory has given rise to a range of techniques that come under the term '**psychoanalysis**'. Freud suggested that some aspects of our personality are unconscious and that our behaviour can be affected by processes of which we are unaware. Freud thought that problems encountered at different stages in our childhoods could have a negative affect on the way we behave as adults, for example, children who encountered difficulties during the oral stage of development could grow up to have addictive-type personalities. Psychoanalysis was developed as a way of helping clients to become aware of some of these unconscious processes with the hope that once a person understood the mechanisms involved, problems could be resolved. Psychoanalysis involves long-term treatment

---

DEFINITION

cognitive behavioural therapy this is a general term for treatments that use behavioural modification techniques together with procedures to change the way individuals think

---

THINK ABOUT IT

Are there any situations that you feel nervous about? Maybe it is waiting for a driving exam or talking to a group of people in public. Perhaps you have a worrying meeting to cope with. Write down your thoughts. For each negative thought try to find a positive one to replace it.

DEFINITION

psychoanalysis the method of treating people with mental disorders based on the theories of Freud and his followers. Psychoanalysis involves helping a client become aware of previously unconscious processes that have affected their behaviour and emotions with clients attending regular therapy sessions, sometimes over a period of years. Freud's theories gave rise to many different theoretical approaches, consequently there are many different versions of psychotherapy, but all involve clients talking about past experiences with a therapist.

Psychoanalysis can be used as a method of treating adults who have suffered a childhood trauma. It is not usually the method of choice for young children because they do not have the ability to be able to express complex feelings and emotions. Instead, therapists have developed a way of working with children through their play. This is known as play therapy.

Play therapy

Play therapy is a way that therapists use to understand children's unconscious feelings. By watching children play, a skilled therapist gains insight into the children's unconscious feelings and will use this knowledge to help the child recognise these feelings for themselves. Once children are aware of their feelings, then they can be helped to deal with them.

Play therapy as a diagnostic tool

There are several different ways of using play as a diagnostic tool. Generally, children are observed playing in a room with the kind of toys you would see in a well-equipped nursery. This would include resources for small world play and drawing and painting material. Sometimes children are observed through a two-way mirror so that they are unaware of being observed. Sometimes children will be left to play on their own, while the therapist observes. Other therapists may prefer to remain with children in the room and comment on what children are doing in an effort to encourage them to express their feelings. By observing children's play and by listening to what

DEFINITION

play therapy   play therapy is a method where children's feelings and emotions can be understood by observing them playing. Play is used as a way of helping children express their feelings and come to terms with life events

Sometimes children are observed playing through a two-way mirror

- Childcare practitioners may observe a child playing in ways that lead the childcare practitioner to suspect that the child has been abused. It is important that this is noted and the establishment's child protection procedures are carried out. Do not be tempted to probe any deeper, as you may, unwittingly, ask leading questions that would make it difficult to use the child's evidence if there was to be a court case. This topic is discussed in more detail in Chapter 4.

- If you are worried about a child who is behaving out of character, observing them at play may help you understand what is affecting them. For example, you may see a child pretending that an older dolly is hitting a baby. If the child had recently gained a baby brother or sister it could indicate that the child is suffering from feelings of jealousy.

counselling a therapy that aims at helping individuals with their personal problems, rather than helping individuals with a mental illness

they say it is possible to understand their feelings and to discover things that have happened to them that they either do not have the language to express, or do not want to talk about directly. If a child is suspected as being the victim of abuse it may be possible to find out who the perpetrator is and what happened to the child.

Using play therapy as a treatment

Play therapy can be used in a variety of ways to help children come to terms with emotions and feelings that they cannot express verbally.

- Children who are coping with painful experiences will relive them in their play. A child who has suffered a bereavement may play at funerals over and over again. Even without the help of a skilled therapist, this sort of play is beneficial to children as it gives them time to come to terms with their feelings. A skilled play therapist will be able to help a child by drawing out their feelings as they play.

- Children, who have very powerful emotions such as anger, may not feel it is safe to express these emotions to their parents. In their play, they can displace these negative emotions on to toys, so that it is not them who are angry, but the pretend people they use in their play who are expressing the anger. A skilled therapist may be able to ask a child playing in this way if they feel angry like the doll, so helping the child express their feelings, which will help them deal with their feelings in a more positive way. In a similar way, children will often express their feelings more easily if they speak through a puppet than if asked to express themselves directly.

- Play therapy can be used to help explain to children complex life events that they would not have the vocabulary to understand. If you were to say to three-year-old children that they were going to hospital for an operation they might not understand, but hospital play specialists can use toys and props to explain to children what will be happening.

- Play therapy can be used by hospital play specialists and childcare practitioners to uncover secret fears that children may have about operations and procedures. Young children often have very distorted beliefs about their bodies and may have worries about harmless procedures. In the same way, children may think that they are to blame for their ill health and play therapy may be able to uncover these hidden beliefs.

Counselling

Psychoanalysis is based on Freudian theory and often involves individuals seeing their therapist for regular sessions over the course of several years. It is unusual for clients to be offered psychotherapy on the National Health Service (NHS) because it is a very expensive use of resources. **Counselling** is a less expensive, shorter and less intensive therapy which is offered on the NHS both in hospitals and in some health centres. Counsellors are often people who work in the caring professions and have undergone extra training. Throughout our lives we will all experience problems and difficulties that cause us emotional pain or upset, such as bereavement, problems with relationships or difficulties at work. Counsellors are trained to help

clients identify and cope with their emotions and to deal constructively with their problems. There is a wide variety of methods used in counselling, but most counselling involves listening to clients and helping them make decisions about what to do, rather than giving clients direct advice. Sometimes counsellors are trained in specific areas such as bereavement counselling, marriage counselling or family counselling. Counsellors work with individual clients or with groups of people.

Because young children often do not have the language to express themselves, counselling is not often used on its own as a therapy for children. Counselling is sometimes offered to parents of children with behaviour difficulties because they may be finding it difficult to come to terms with their child's condition or because of the stress of looking after their child.

Family therapy

Sometimes the behavioural difficulties in children can be seen to have their origins in problems within the family unit. If parents are having marital problems and are having violent rows, the children may refuse to go to school for fear of leaving their mother on her own with their father, or a young child's temper tantrums may be being reinforced by the attention he receives from the adults who care for him.

In family therapy, it is usual for two therapists, one male and one female, to work with the family. During sessions, the family and therapists meet together and the therapists observe the family to see how they interact and respond to each other. The therapists try to help the family members

---

CASE STUDY

Mr and Mrs Smith have two children, a boy, Rory, aged 8 years and a girl, Jenny, aged 6 years. Recently, Mrs Smith gave birth to a baby who was very ill and lived only for a week. Within the family, both parents find it impossible to talk to each other about their grief. Nobody has explained to the children what happened and the children were not taken to the funeral of their baby brother. The children are afraid to talk to their parents about the baby because they do not want to make their mother cry and their father is always angry now. On the day the baby was born, Jenny was due to go to a friend's party but she was unable to go because she was sent to her grandma's house. Jenny was cross and told her grandmother that she wished the baby had not been born. Jenny half thinks that, if she hadn't said this, the baby would be still alive. Jenny thinks her father's anger is directed at her. Jenny has started to wet the bed and is refusing to go to school.

1 Taking each family member in turn, describe how he or she might be feeling.

2 There is not much communication going on within the family. What are the negative effects of this?

3 Why might Jenny be wetting the bed?

4 If you were working with this family, how might you help them?

understand how their actions and reactions contribute to the family's problems. Video recordings are often used to demonstrate how individuals react. Video recordings of parents interacting with their children in the home situation have been used to demonstrate how parental actions are causing the problem behaviour with the children. Often parents are unaware of the effect that their behaviour is having and, once recognised, the parents can begin to work on strategies to help overcome the family's difficulties.

Music therapy

Music therapy has been used successfully, for over fifty years, to help people with physical and mental illness and those with learning difficulties. It has also been particularly successful in helping individuals who have an autistic spectrum disorder. Music has a universal appeal and, however profound an individual's difficulties, very few fail to respond to music. The universal appeal is likely to be connected with the rhythms in our bodies. We feel the regular beat of our hearts and, as a baby in our mother's womb, we heard the regular rhythm of her heartbeat. One can hear melody in human speech and conversations are based on turn taking, in the same way as in music making. This responsiveness to music can be used to build a relationship between the therapist and the client. Music therapy is different from teaching individuals to play an instrument, although children may learn during the course of music therapy. Music therapy can be carried out in a number of ways.

- A music therapist may play music to match the emotions of the client. An agitated child may be soothed by hearing restful music, while loud, turbulent music may help a child express feelings of anger.

- Therapists can use musical improvisation. They may give children a musical instrument such as a drum and wait for the child to make a sound with it. The therapist will then reply to the sound on her own instrument, either by copying the sound or using the sound in an **improvisation**. If children do not, or are not, able to use an instrument, the therapist will respond to the children's voices. The therapist will pause to allow the child to reply, in his own way, and gradually a musical conversation is developed.

- A music therapist may use simple melodies and songs that are repeated throughout the sessions, as a response to changing moods and emotions.

- Music therapy sessions can be held on an individual or group basis, and are always structured, as far as possible, to be held at the same time and place each week. This consistency is especially important for children who have Autistic Spectrum Disorder (ASD).

- Music therapy has been reported to have a variety of benefits.

- It improves social interaction because it encourages children to listen, respond to other people and take turns.

- Music therapy can encourage children to use their voices to communicate which encourages language development.

- Music therapy increases children's attention span and can help them develop shared attention, that is the ability to attend to the same thing, at the same time, as someone else. This is part of the ability to interact successfully with others.

- Music therapy can help children express emotions and recognise the emotions of others.

- Listening to music with very young children has been shown to improve mother-child interaction, which is the basis of future social interaction.

- Music therapy can encourage children with limited mobility to use their muscles to produce a sound from a musical instrument.

- Listening to music is relaxing and can reduce stress, which will have benefits on all areas of learning.

Art and drama therapy

Art therapy and drama therapy can be used in a way similar to play therapy in that they can be both a diagnostic and a therapeutic tool.

Art therapy

In art therapy, children are encouraged to use a variety of media. A skilled art therapist can recognise a child's emotions and feelings in their artistic creations and can use this either to help in their understanding of what is worrying a child, or as a way of helping children understand and express their emotions.

- Art therapy can be relaxing. Using clay or finger painting, in particular, can be soothing.

- Children can express feelings of anger and frustration by painting violent pictures or by aggressive use of clay and other materials.

- By interpreting a child's emotions, a therapist can help a child come to terms with their feelings.

Finger painting can be soothing

GOOD PRACTICE

Try to keep a record of the content of children's art work. Although one picture may not reveal much about a child, you may detect a pattern that can reveal a troubled mind. Children in the middle of war situations may compulsively draw the violent scenes they have witnessed.

- Children can relive experiences in their art work that they may not be able to express in other ways.
- Art therapy allows very young children, without adequate language, to explain their feelings.

Drama therapy

There are two main methods used in drama therapy – psychodrama and role play.

- Psychodrama involves the use of drama to help children act out key events in their lives. This is a natural part of play for young children, where you may see them re-enacting an event such as going to hospital or a wedding they have just been to. Acting out events helps children come to terms with what has happened and can help them express feelings and emotions that they find difficult.

- Role play is used to act out situations that may be a challenge for children. Children can practice asking for things politely, rather than demanding things in an aggressive way. Those who lack social skills can practice how to greet someone. Role play has been used to help children practise what they would say if they were offered a cigarette, or how to cope with bullies. In group situations, role play can be used to help children understand the effects their behaviour is having on others and can help them understand what others may be feeling.

✔ PROGRESS CHECK

1 When might psychosurgery be used on children?
2 Name a behavioural condition in children which may be treated by drugs.
3 When giving medication to children what safety points do you have to take into consideration?
4 What is the difference between behaviour therapy and behaviour modification?
5 Outline a behaviour modification programme for a three-year-old child who clings to his key worker and refuses to join in with the other children.
6 How can play therapy be used to help a child who has recently been bereaved?
7 What are the benefits of music therapy?
8 Why is family therapy often more successful than treating children on their own?

THE WORK OF FAMILY CENTRES

In many areas, there are family centres set up by the local social services departments, often in conjunction with the local education authority. Family centres aim to help mothers and fathers overcome difficulties encountered when caring for children. The centres provide advice, guidance and practical help for parents so that parents can learn how to recognise and meet the needs of babies and young children. The centres can advise parents on how to cope with their children's temper tantrums, how to establish bedtime routines and how to overcome feeding difficulties.

Many parents who are helped by family centres are referred by health visitors, GPs or social workers but most centres hold drop-in sessions for any parent who needs help. Centres vary in the facilities they offer. The following section outlines the most common services offered by family centres.

Family sessions

Family sessions involve parents and children attending the centre for usually for one or two sessions a week. Although each centre will run sessions differently it is usual for four to six families to attend with two or more members of staff being available. The staff, usually highly trained and experienced childcare practitioners, work with the parents and produce highly focused plans so that staff and parents know exactly what are the aims of the sessions and the goals they are working towards.

Sessions can be used for a variety of purposes.

- Helping parents set consistent boundaries for their children.
- Exploring ways of disciplining children without smacking or shouting.
- Helping parents to have realistic expectations for their children.
- Helping parents establish appropriate daily routines and routines for mealtimes and bedtimes.
- Looking at accident prevention and safety within the home.
- Helping parents relate to their children. Looking at establishing eye contact, non-directive play and games parents can play with their children.
- Assisting parents in planning and preparing meals and budgeting.

Sometimes family sessions are used if children are on the child protection register as a way of supporting parents who may be at risk of having their children taken away.

Parenting courses

In addition to family sessions, centres may offer parenting courses. These courses are often available for any parent who feels that they would benefit from support and guidance in caring for their children. Centres will also accept referrals from health visitors, teachers, GPs, speech therapists and social workers. Typically, a parenting group will meet weekly and be run by an experienced childcare practitioner. The topics covered will be similar to those covered in family sessions except that the children will not be part of the class. There is usually crèche provision provided. In the classes, parents are encouraged to share their experiences with others to help them to understand that the difficulties that they face as parents are not unusual. Some centres will devise their own parenting programme, while others will use published material as a basis for the sessions.

Nursery sessions

Most family centres run nursery sessions for children. Depending on the centre, these sessions may be full time or part time. Sometimes the nursery is part of a large early years childcare and education centre, while other centres run sessions specifically for children who have been referred by health visitors, GPs, social workers or from speech therapists. Children who attend these sessions are normally those who would benefit from being in a small group and who may have special learning or behavioural needs.

After-school sessions

After-school sessions are run by some centres. These are usually for children of primary school age who have been identified as having social needs and who would benefit from being in a small group. Referrals are usually from health visitors, teachers, social workers and speech therapists. Sessions are designed to focus on the individual needs of the children. Within a small group, there is an opportunity for staff to work intensively with children, looking at exploring feelings in a safe environment and learning how to build relationships with adults and other children.

Individual sessions with parents

Sometimes it is more appropriate for childcare practitioners to work with parents on their own. This can be at the centre or in the parent's home. Sessions focus on the same issues as in family sessions, but more intensive work can be undertaken on a one-to-one basis. The sessions may involve using a video camera to record the interaction between the parent and the

Sometimes mother and child interactions are recorded on video

child. Afterwards, the childcare practitioner will discuss the video with the parent and help them see how his or her own actions may precipitate difficult behaviour in the child. Working one-to-one with parents in their own house can help parents establish bedtime routines or appropriate behaviour management techniques.

Individual play sessions for children

- Children who are experiencing difficulties may be given the opportunity to play within a centre or in their own home for a session a week over a fixed period of time. In these sessions, a childcare practitioner or other professional such as a play therapist or social worker, will use a variety of age appropriate play materials to engage the child in positive play experiences. The sessions may be designed to:
- help children build positive relationships with adults
- help children understand their family history or life story if they are in care
- give children a positive experience of play if this has been denied them through poor parenting or other circumstances such as illness
- help children to relax and enable them to express their emotions in a safe environment.

CASE STUDY

Jo is a single mother living on the ninth floor of a run-down high-rise development. She has two children, a three-year-old and a baby of 9 months. Since the birth of her baby, Jo has become increasingly depressed. The demands of the children are too much for her and her health visitor is worried that she is shouting and smacking the children far too often. The children have no routine and the three-year-old is very difficult around meal times and bedtimes. Jo is receiving medical help from her GP. Jo finds it very difficult to take the children out to the park to play as she has so little energy. Her three-year-old child is not attending a nursery. She has been told that the local nursery school will take her when she is 3½ years old. The health visitor refers Jo for family sessions at the local family centre.

1 What aspects of parenting might the staff concentrate on in the family session?
2 What facility might be offered for the three-year-old?
3 Why might Jo find it very difficult to attend family sessions and what might be offered to help her?

Additional services

Family centres may offer additional services such as

- toy libraries which may supply toys for children with disabilities

KEY TERMS

You need to know the meaning
of the following words and
phrases. Go back through the
chapter to make sure you
understand them:

behaviour modification
behaviour therapy
cognitive behavioural
  therapy
counselling
improvisation
play therapy
primary health care
psychoanalysis
psychotherapy
screening
surveillance
systematic desensitisation

- contact centres where parents can be given supervised access to their children as a result of court procedures

- drop-in sessions for victims of domestic abuse

- drop-in centres where any parents can bring their children so that children can have the opportunity to play. Parents can get support and advice about parenting skills and information about children''s services. There may be different drop-ins for parents with toddlers and babies.

FURTHER READING

Axline, V. (1971) *Dibs in Search of Self*, Pelican Books
    There are several good books about play therapy. This is a classic and is strongly recommended for students studying at all levels.
Axline, V. (1989) *Play Therapy*, Churchill Livingstone
Bancroft, D. and Carr, R. (1995) *Influencing Children's Development*, Blackwell in association with The Open University
    Chapter 18 in this book is an excellent chapter on therapies.
Graham, P. (1998) *Cognitive Behaviour Therapy for Children and Families*, Cambridge University Press
Hobart, C. and Frankel, J. (1998) *A Practical Guide to Child Observation and Assessment*, Stanley Thornes
Lindon, J. (2001) *Understanding Children's Play*, Nelson Thornes
Quinn, M. and Quinn, T. (1995) *From Pram to Primary School: Parenting Small Children from Birth to Age Six or Seven*, The Family Caring Trust UK
    This a programme that can be used to help parents with parenting skills within family centres.
West, J. (1996) *Child Centred Play Therapy* (2nd edition), Arnold

Most good introductory text books on psychology have a section on therapies. These books are especially recommended.
Atkinson, R.C., Atkinson, R., Smith, E., Bem, D. and Nolen-Hoeksema, S. (1996) *Hilgard's Introduction to Psychology* (International edition), Harcourt Brace
Davenport, G. (1994) *An Introduction to Child Development*, Collins Educational

6

Common causes of concern

PREVIEW

This chapter includes:

- Eating
- Sleeping
- Bed wetting and soiling
- Temper tantrums
- Difficulties in getting on with others
- Habits
- Antisocial behaviour (swearing, lying, stealing).

It is a very rare child who passes through infancy and childhood without exhibiting some sort of behaviour that worries the adults who care for them. In this chapter, we will be looking at some of the more common causes of concern. When considering what to do when confronted with a child who is worrying us we need, first of all, to take into account the child's age. It is not normal for a seven-year-old child to have frequent temper tantrums, whereas it is common in a two-year-old child.

Another principle to apply, when thinking about how to manage any of the behaviours outlined in this chapter, is that the adult should try to remain relaxed. An anxious, stressed adult is more likely to make things worse, despite his or her best intentions.

THINK ABOUT IT

Imagine the following scenes.

● It is Christmas day. The mother has been planning her Christmas dinner since October when she made the Christmas puddings. All day she has been cooking the meal, putting all her love and energy into providing the best ever Christmas for her family. Meanwhile the children have been opening their presents and have been eating some of the sweets they have been given. When dinner is served they do not want to eat. They want to play with their toys. The parents insist that they join the family at the table and there are tears.

● A childcare practitioner is sitting with a group of three-year-olds while they are eating their lunch. One of the items is broccoli. She turns to her colleague and says, 'Ugh! I could never eat that!' The children look at her. Two refuse to eat their broccoli and the childcare practitioner tells them that they must eat it all up.

● It is a cold, snowy day. The children are home from school, being cared for by their father. Mother puts on her coat to go to work. One of the children says to her, 'Don't go to work today Mum, stay at home and make soup.'

All three scenes show that eating and food is often surrounded with emotions. Which emotions can you identify?

A tea party at Christmas

EATING

When looking at the first and last scenes, I expect you could identify that both adults and children associate the making of food with love. If this food is rejected it may feel as if the person who made the food is being rejected.

The sharing of food together is also full of social significance. Most special occasions, whatever the culture, are marked by the sharing of food and drink. Many religious ceremonies also involve people eating and drinking together.

Children can pick up negative attitudes about food by the reaction of people around them, for example the childcare practitioner giving negative messages about broccoli (see page 136). Sometimes, in our society where it is seen to be important that we are slim and beautiful, children can begin to think that enjoying food is 'bad' or they feel guilty eating some foods such as chocolate. Some children as young as 7 years have been found to be 'dieting' because they think they are fat. Because there are so many complex emotions around eating, it is hardly surprising that many children give cause for concern over their eating behaviour.

The following section looks at two common concerns about children's eating: the child who is a reluctant eater and the child who is overweight. In both cases, the advice is for children over 1 year of age. If you have concerns about a baby under 1 year of age, professional advice must be sought.

It is natural for children's appetites to change from time to time. After an illness, it may take a while for a child to start eating normally. Children, like adults, may have likes and dislikes in food and it would be unreasonable to expect them to like everything. Many parents worry that their child eats too little, or are concerned that the child eats a very limited diet. Children have been known to put themselves on diets consisting of milk and jam sandwiches.

Parents and carers can be reassured that it is very rare for such children to come to any physical harm because of their eating patterns.

Guidelines for reluctant eaters

- Restrict the amount of food children eat between meals to a piece of fruit. Offer water, milk or diluted fruit juices to drink.
- Plenty of fresh air and exercise will stimulate the appetite.

Family and friends enjoying a meal together

THINK ABOUT IT

What are the consequences to a child's all-round development if they do not get sufficient sleep?

Children who do not get enough sleep may be tired and fretful during the day time. They will be less able to relate to others socially and could either show signs of withdrawal, or become aggressive towards others. Lack of sleep will make learning more difficult because the child will have less energy to explore and will have a poor concentration span. Physically, a child may become susceptible to infections and have a poor appetite, leading to poor growth.

It is also important for the adults who care for children that the children get sufficient sleep. Caring for a sleep-deprived child is often difficult and in addition parents/carers benefit from having some time to themselves when the child is sleeping.

The child who is reluctant to go to bed

The time that children go to bed and where and with whom they sleep are socially and culturally determined. In many families in Britain, it is assumed that young children of about 5 years will go to bed at around 7 o'clock and will sleep in their own bed, in a room that is separate from that of their parents. In some countries, it is usual for young children stay up until much later and sleep in the same room as the parents, often in the same bed. These children are likely to have a considerable sleep in the afternoon. In situations where there is no artificial light, the whole family is likely to go to bed as night falls, rising at dawn.

In a situation where children are expected to go to bed leaving older children and adults still up, they may feel that they are missing something exciting, or they may feel rejected. This is especially true if they go to bed in a room all on their own (a practice that is considered cruel in some societies). Many children at some time will protest at going to bed. In some households, bedtime becomes a time of stress and heightened emotions. The children may refuse to go to bed or exhibit behaviours such as crying and temper tantrums. Adults may lose their temper and shout or even smack the children. With a little time and energy, however, most bedtime problems can be resolved.

Guidelines to help children go to bed happily

These guidelines are for parents, carers and childcare practitioners working as nannies. The advice is relevant for children over 1 year old. For specific advice about babies, a health visitor should be consulted.

- Consider whether adult expectations are realistic. A bedtime that is too early for a child who is not tired will be difficult to enforce.
- Ensure that the child has had sufficient exercise during the day. Exercise will induce a healthy tiredness.
- It often helps if the child's main meal is in the middle of the day. Eating a big meal too near bedtime may hinder sleep.
- A consistent bedtime routine is important. Children will feel a sense of security if they know what is going to happen to them.
- The last part of the child's day should be for quiet play to help the child 'unwind'.
- An evening bath is relaxing. Adults should give the child all of their attention and not rush things because of other household chores.

TRY THIS!

If you are a childcare practitioner or a student in a childcare establishment, ask the parents of the children in your care what time the children go to bed at night time. The more parents you ask, the more realistic a picture you will get of average bedtimes for different ages of children.

If you are doing this exercise as part of a group at college you could pool your results and represent your findings graphically.

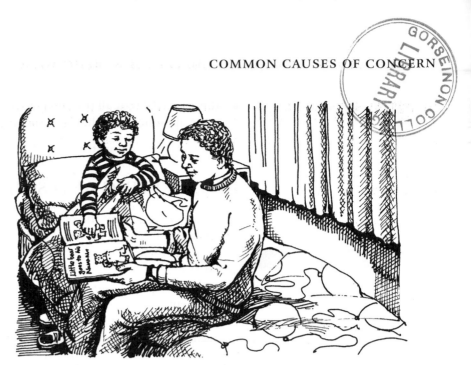

A bedtime story is comforting

- A milky drink before bed often helps a child sleep, as long as the child's teeth are cleaned afterwards.
- When the child is ready for bed let him choose a story book for the adult to read to him.
- When it's time for bed, care must be taken to make the bed and the room as comfortable as possible.
- The room should be well ventilated with a night light or dimmer switch. Many children do not want to sleep in the dark.
- Ensure that the child has his favourite toy and any comfort object that he uses. Some children will like a drink of water within reach.
- When the child is in bed and has had his goodnight kiss and a cuddle, tell him that it is bedtime and that you will be downstairs or wherever you will be.
- If the child cries, leave him for a minute or two, return to him and from the door tell him that you are there, but it is bedtime. Never go back into the room and give him another cuddle. This way, you will be showing the child that he hasn't been abandoned, but that he is expected to sleep.
- If the child gets out of bed and comes to find you, gently lead him back, put him into bed with as little fuss as possible. Tell him again that it is bedtime and you expect him to stay in bed.
- If you are trying to help a child who has been in the habit of playing up at bedtime, you may find that the first week of the new regime is tiring. If you persevere and do not lose your temper, you should find that the child gradually finds bedtimes easier to cope with.
- Never give in and allow the child to stay up longer, or give him extra cuddles or stories and so on. That way, you will be rewarding the very behaviour that you want to stop. Use the positive behaviour management strategies described in Chapter 4.

GOOD PRACTICE

Occasionally there may be a physical reason why a child protests at going to bed. Children with eczema may find the irritation is worse in bed. Children with intestinal worms may find going to sleep difficult because the worms cause irritation around the anus.

Parents should seek advice from a health visitor or GP if simple remedies to help the child sleep do not help.

not to co-operate. This can lead to a child's behaviour giving cause for concern.

Problem behaviour

Examples of problem behaviour are:

- refusing to use the potty
- hiding out of sight to deposit a bowel motion, for instance under a table or behind a curtain, when you know that he is able to use the potty
- passing a bowel motion only when his nappy is put on at night time
- withholding bowel motions for several days. If this happens, chronic constipation can occur. Occasionally, the child will soil themselves because more fluid faeces leak out around the hard stool and parents/carers may think the child has diarrhoea.

Guidelines for helping a child who soils or who withholds his bowel movement

- Keep relaxed about the situation. Believe that the child will adopt socially acceptable behaviour in his own time.
- Do not get into a power struggle with the child.
- Put the child back into nappies, not as a punishment, but to take the pressure off. Wait a few more weeks before trying again.
- If the child is constipated because of withholding their bowel motion add more fruit to the child's diet, especially fruit such as plums and prunes. Increase the amount of water that you give the child to drink.

GOOD PRACTICE

If the simple measures to treat constipation, outlined in the text, do not work, parents should ask the health visitor or GP for advice. Never give children over-the-counter remedies for constipation.

✔ PROGRESS CHECK

1 Give three possible causes of bedwetting.
2 What does it mean to say that a child has regressed?
3 Outline the guidelines for helping a child who has enuresis.
4 If a child is constipated what action should you take?

TEMPER TANTRUMS

Temper tantrums are a common feature of childhood. They are characterised by bouts of uncontrollable rage and can be distressing to watch if you are unfamiliar with this aspect of children's behaviour. They are caused by a build-up of frustration, to a point where the child can no longer contain the strong emotion that he feels.

Incidence of temper tantrums

More than half of all two-year-olds will have a temper tantrum at least once a day. It is very rare for a child to have reached his third birthday without experiencing a tantrum. From 3 years onwards, the incidence of tantrums diminishes, as children's ability to communicate improves and they achieve more self-control. Frequent temper tantrums in an older child are a cause for concern and professional advice should be sought.

Behavioural characteristics of temper tantrums

Children can vary in the behaviour they show during a tantrum but usually each child tends to behave consistently, that is they show the similar behaviour on each occasion. The following are behaviours that are frequently seen:

- rushing around the room, screaming
- throwing himself on the floor, kicking and screaming
- screaming until he makes himself sick, or turns blue in the face
- holding his breath until he almost loses consciousness
- going as stiff as a board.
- using words and expressive jargon to express emotion.

Causes of temper tantrums

The main cause of temper tantrums is a build-up of frustration within a child together with the inability to exercise self-control due to the child's emotional and cognitive immaturity.

When you carried out the 'Think about it' exercise, I expect you were able to identify several situations that lead to frustration. Common causes include the following.

- The struggle for independence. The child strives to do things for himself. It is this need for independence that is one of the driving forces of the child's development, but often the child wants to do something that is beyond his capabilities and the frustration builds up. The child may want to fasten up his shoes and is frustrated when he is unable to do so.

- Frustration when the child feels that the adults who are caring for him are controlling his behaviour. Almost any aspect of everyday life can cause this kind of frustration, from using the potty, going to bed or mealtimes. Toddlers are very good at detecting when an issue is important to the carer. For instance, if it is important that today the child eats his lunch quickly so that you can go out, it will be this occasion that the child will refuse. It is always wise to anticipate a potential trigger and act as if you had all the time in the world.

- Frustration because of their size and strength. Toddlers will become frustrated because they can't do things their older brothers and sisters can. They can't run as fast, kick the ball as well, reach the swing and so on. Where possible, parents/carers should choose equipment that is within the child's capabilities.

Guidelines for handling temper tantrums

- Do not allow yourself to get angry. Do not argue or scream back. The child is out of control and frightened by what is happening. Your anger or aggression will only make things worse. Never smack a child in an attempt to stop a temper tantrum.

THINK ABOUT IT

What may build up levels of frustration in a two-year-old toddler?

Do you want to use the red toothbrush or the yellow one?

- Make sure that the child is safe. If the child is running around uncontrollably or thrashing on the ground, remove objects that may hurt him.
- If the child will let you, gently hold him so that he feels safe. If holding the child makes him worse, wait until the temper has subsided and then give him a cuddle. The child will be very frightened and will need to know that you still love him and that he is all right.
- Once the tantrum has subsided, comfort the child. Do not reward the child by giving in to his demands, or punish him for his loss of control.
- Use these guidelines even in public places such as the supermarket. Temper tantrums are a normal part of growing up and you should not feel that you should give in to a toddler's demands in an effort to get him to behave in a public place.

Helping children learn self-control

Between the ages of 3 and 5 years, it is appropriate to give the child a minute or two of 'time out' for him to cool down and regain his composure. This may be just waiting with him until he calms down and then carrying on as usual, or suggesting that he spends a few minutes alone until he has calmed down. This should not be seen as a punishment and it is essential that the adult does not aggressively drag the child to his room. It should be seen as something we all do if we need to cool off. Always praise children if they have handled a frustrating situation well.

School-age children can be helped by giving them strategies to help them control their actions. One method is to suggest the child visualises a red 'stop' light. This then gives the child the opportunity to consider the possible results of their actions. Children can also be taught how to relax and take a few deep breaths. Role play is a useful tool that gives children the opportunity to practise strategies that will help them gain self-control, such as walking away from conflict situations.

✔ PROGRESS CHECK

- Outline the causes of temper tantrums.
- How can you reduce the incidence of temper tantrums?
- Describe how you would handle a child who was having a temper tantrum.

Consider the relationships you have with others in your own life and how the quality of these relationships can affect your feeling of wellbeing.

DIFFICULTIES IN GETTING ON WITH OTHERS

The development of social skills is an important aspect of growing up. Most adults would agree that the quality of the relationships in our lives is a big factor in how happy and fulfilled we feel.

Children start to learn how to relate to others from the moment they are born. In Chapter 2, we looked at the processes of bonding and attachment and it was noted that, if all does not go well, a child may find forming satisfying relationships difficult.

Learning how to get on with others

Children learn how to relate to others in the same way that they learn other skills.

- They watch to see how others do it. Parents, childcare practitioners and older children are all used as role models for children.
- They experiment to see the effect their behaviour has on others.
- They will tend to repeat behaviour that is rewarded.
- They will tend to stop behaviour that fails to gain them a reward.

These points will be used in the next section where we will be looking at various behaviours that children may exhibit while learning how to relate to others.

Aggression

Children of different ages act aggressively in different ways. Younger children may bite or push, older ones may hit or kick. Sometimes, aggression is the result of frustration; for instance, a child may see a toy that another child is playing with and will make an aggressive act to get what he wants. Often such aggression is because the child has yet to develop the language and social skills to cope in any other way. Sometimes, seemingly aggressive acts may be part of toddlers' explorations about the world around them. Childcare practitioners may be familiar with the situation where a toddler gives another toddler a shove just to see what will happen. The resulting fuss and attention may amaze the child, who will repeat it to see what happens the next time. There is a danger that such experimentation might lead to an established behaviour pattern because the child is rewarded by the attention given to him by adults, even though this is negative attention. Unfortunately, some behaviour can be learned from other children or adults. A child may kick

TRY THIS!

Choose a child in your workplace or training placement to observe whose behaviour is giving cause for concern, such as biting, hitting or pushing other children. Carry out an observation where you record every instance of aggression over a period of a few days. For each instance, record what happened. Also record the events immediately preceding the aggression, that triggered the aggressive act. In addition, record what happened immediately after the event. This kind of observation is known as an event sample. Analyse your results. Can you see a pattern? Can you identify things that are likely to trigger the child's aggression? If so, you may be able to think of ways of avoiding trouble. You may be able to identify actions by the childcare practitioners that are unwittingly rewarding the child's behaviour. The child may get lots of attention whenever they hit someone, or they may be allowed to keep the toy that they have made another child give up by being aggressive.

somebody because they have just seen someone else do it. They are more likely to imitate such behaviour if the child whom they observed got what he wanted by kicking, or was not disciplined. Children will also learn to hit if they see other children or adults hitting.

How to help a child who exhibits aggressive behaviour

- If you see a child being aggressive to another child, briefly observe the situation to see if the children can resolve their dispute. If the situation does not resolve, look the child in the eye and firmly say something like, 'No hitting'.
- Make sure that the child who has been hit is comforted.
- Do not let the child benefit in any way from his behaviour. If he wanted the other child's toy, make sure that he does not get it.
- If the child goes into a temper tantrum, ignore him until he has calmed down. (Use the guidelines for handling temper tantrums that were discussed previously.)
- In a quiet moment, explain why such behaviour is not allowed.
- Help the child find more appropriate ways of getting what he wants. For instance, asking nicely or getting an adult to help.
- Help the victim find appropriate ways of dealing with a similar situation in future. Teach him to say loudly, 'Don't hit me. I don't like it', rather than giving in to the other child, or using aggressive behaviour back.
- Make sure that children do not see adults acting aggressively, because they will copy this behaviour.

Biting

Biting is a behaviour that particularly worries parents but many children bite when they are very young. A baby uses his mouth as a way of exploring the environment and biting is an aspect of this exploration. Some babies find biting relieves the discomfort of teething and biting can also be a response to excitement. Although biting at this age is not a concern, it is sensible to redirect the behaviour early on. For instance, if the baby bites you, it is appropriate for you to tell him that you do not like it and to give him something more appropriate to bite, such as a teething ring.

Between 13 and 30 months, the incidence of biting tends to increase and should stop around 3 years of age. Toddlers mainly bite out of frustration, for instance if another child has the toy that they want, and is a problem when you have a group of toddlers being looked after together in a nursery. When biting occurs in nurseries, the situation is compounded because parents are involved. The parent of the biter may worry that their child may be asked to leave, and the nursery staff will have the unpleasant task of explaining to the parent of the child who was bitten what has happened. If the incidents are regular, the parents of the other children may demand that action is taken.

Guidelines on how to help a child who bites

- Help the child understand that biting is forbidden. When a child bites, look him in the eye and say, firmly, something like, 'No biting' or 'Stop biting. That hurts'. Avoid lengthy explanations as this may reward the behaviour by giving the child extra attention.

- Make sure that the child does not think biting is a game. Never laugh, even if the biting is playful. Adults should avoid giving playful nips to the child, the child will not understand why your 'play bites' are all right while his are not.

- If one child bites another, separate them and say, 'No biting'. Do not be aggressive towards the child and never bite him back. This only tells the child that biting is acceptable. Comfort the child who has been bitten.

- Teach the child who is biting more appropriate ways of communicating what they want. For instance, if another child has something that he wants, you could teach him to point to it and ask for it nicely, or to ask an adult for help.

- When you see the child using the strategies that you have taught him, give praise and encouragement.

- Be a good role model. If children see adults using aggressive behaviour they will copy this.

- Seek professional help if these measures do not improve the situation.

GOOD PRACTICE

- If a child bites you never bite back.
- In a nursery situation, **all** childcare practitioners should apply the guidelines consistently. An inconsistent approach may prolong the behaviour.

CASE STUDY

Peter is 23 months old and attends the workplace nursery attached to a hospital. Recently he has started biting other children if they have something he wants. His mother, Pat, is a nurse in the hospital. She is a single parent. Peter is her only child. Pat is very worried because yesterday Peter bit the son of one of the hospital managers. The manager approached both her and the officer in charge of the nursery, demanding that action must be taken. The hospital manager implied that if the matter was not resolved then Pat should look elsewhere for a place for Peter. Pat is worried that she may have to give up her job as other nurseries in the area are too expensive for her.

1 What action could the officer in charge of the nursery take to help Peter reduce his biting?

2 How could Pat help Peter at home?

3 How should the officer in charge handle to situation between the hospital manager and Pat?

Learning to share

Very young children are not able to share because they are, by nature, self-centred. It is only as they grow older that they are begin to understand that not everything belongs to them. The concept of 'mine' is not learned until about 15 months and, although by 3 years old children begin to understand about sharing, childcare practitioners will be aware that quarrels over sharing persist throughout childhood. Parents can help toddlers understand that not all possessions belong to the child by pointing out 'Mummy's hat' or

'Daddy's drink'. Possessions such bags and gloves can be used to help young children begin to understand what is theirs and what belongs to someone else. As children begin to mix with other children, there will inevitably be squabbles about sharing. Sometimes, adults will need to intervene, especially if one child is using aggressive behaviour, but it is a good idea to watch what happens first. Children need the opportunity to learn how to deal with these situations for themselves without too much adult interference. If adults always sort out children's disputes, they will not learn how to do this for themselves.

Dealing with disputes over sharing

- If one child has taken a nursery toy from another child and the children have not been able to resolve the situation themselves, give the toy back to the first child. Tell the other child they can play with the toy in a little while.

- Sometimes you do not know who had the toy first. If neither child will give up the toy, take it away and interest both children in something else.

- Use a timer for very popular toys. When the timer goes off, the child playing with the toy knows that he has to hand it over to the other child.

- If the toy belongs to a child and they refuse to let the other child play with it, distract the child who wanted it with something more interesting. The owner of the toy may feel more like sharing later on. You might be able to tell them how grown up it is to be able to share toys.

- Never force a child to share possessions if they are not ready to do so. It is better to use praise and encouragement as a reward for when they do share than to use punishment when they do not.

✔ PROGRESS CHECK

1 Describe the ways in which a child might learn aggressive behaviour.
2 Outline how to deal with a child who bites other children in a nursery.
3 How can we help young children share nursery toys?

DEFINITION
habit a behaviour pattern that is repeated over and over again until it becomes automatic

HABITS

Habits are well-established behaviour patterns and for the most part they are beneficial. Childcare practitioners want to teach children good hygiene habits such as hand washing after going to the lavatory, or teeth cleaning after meals. These activities are often incorporated into nursery routines.

Some habits, such as nail biting or thumb sucking are habits that are comforting for the child but are a source of annoyance or concern for the parents/carers.

Common habits that concern adults are:

- thumb sucking
- nail biting

- hair twirling
- nose picking
- breath holding
- masturbation.

Thumb sucking

Babies have been shown to suck their thumb even before they are born and it is one of the most common childhood habits. It is thought that the habit starts when the baby accidentally finds his thumb with his mouth and occasionally babies will suck one or more fingers instead. Thumb sucking is very common; 45 per cent of two-year-olds suck their thumb, but the habit dies out as children grow older. By the age of 11, only 5 per cent of children suck their thumb.

Nail biting

Nail biting, or picking at the fingers, is also very common in children. Between the ages of 5 and 18 it is estimated that 40 per cent of children bite their nails. Most often children bite their finger nails, but some bite their toe nails. Although in early childhood, boys and girls equally bite their nails, boys are more likely to engage in the habit as they get older.

Hair twirling

Hair can be twisted, stroked or pulled and is a behaviour seen most often in girls. The habit usually appears in early childhood and can persist until adolescence and beyond. The majority of hair twirlers are girls and, in extreme cases it can result in bald patches.

Hair twirling is more common in girls

Nose picking

Nose picking is a habit that starts in childhood and can persist until adulthood.

Breath holding

This can be a frightening habit for parents to experience, but is unlikely to cause the child any harm. Breath holding can start as early as 6 months old and is often seen in tense, overactive children. Breath holding sometimes leads to the child passing out, whereupon they resume breathing. Very occasionally breath holding may precipitate a seizure. Breath holding is often seen in children who are frustrated and are not able to get their own way.

Masturbation

It is normal for children to explore their bodies around the second year, when they are no longer wearing nappies during the day. Boys learn that they get pleasurable feelings when they play with their penis and girls may insert their fingers into their vagina. Sometimes children rock as they rub themselves. Masturbation is only a cause for concern if children choose to comfort themselves in this way to such an extent that they do not participate in normal nursery activities, or they masturbate in situations where it is socially unacceptable. Excessive masturbation may indicate that a child has been sexually abused. Chapter 4 looks at child protection issues.

Causes of habits

Experts are not always sure what causes a habit but, whatever the cause, the child must be receiving some benefit, otherwise the habit would not have become established.

- All the habits described, except breath holding are comfort behaviours. They soothe children and are often seen if children are anxious.
- Sometimes there may be a familial or genetic influence, especially in nail biting.
- Habits may arise because of boredom or lack of stimulation. Thumb sucking and masturbation are often a response to lack of stimulation.
- Thumb sucking has its origins in infancy, when babies get pleasurable feelings from sucking. Hair twirling may also have its origins in infancy since many infants play with their mother's hair during feeding.
- Breath holding may be a way of attracting attention and is a powerful way of manipulating parents because the behaviour is so frightening.

How to help children overcome their habits

Although parents are often worried about their children's habits, a relaxed approach is very likely to be the most sensible way of dealing with the problem. Most children, left to their own devices, will grow out of the habit. Sometimes more active steps may need to be taken, for instance if a child's teeth are being affected by thumb sucking, or the child is being teased by other children at school. The following measures have been found to be helpful.

- Do not draw undue notice to the habit, too much pressure to stop can make the habit harder to break.
- Gently talk to the child and explain why you do not like the habit. For instance you could explain that thumb sucking is pushing her teeth out of place.
- Ask for the child's ideas as to what you can do to help them break the habit. Putting the child in control is more likely to lead to success than if you impose your ideas on them.
- Reward the child when they show self-control. For instance if the child usually bites her nails when looking at the television, you could mention that you had noticed that she hardly bit her nails during a particular programme and congratulate her.
- Children may like to choose some nice nail polish to put on their nails as they grow.
- There are products available to put on thumbs or nails that make them taste nasty. These sometimes work in the short term, but persistent thumb suckers or nail bitters may well put up with the taste.
- Breath holding is best responded to by ignoring it. If the child does not get what she wants by holding her breath, the behaviour will soon disappear. Some of the suggestions for helping children who have temper tantrums will also be helpful.
- Review the child's day, keep boredom at bay and try to reduce any stress the child may be experiencing.

✔ PROGRESS CHECK

1 At what age is thumb sucking most common?
2 Give three reasons why children may develop habits.
3 How could you help a child stop biting her nails?
4 What advice would you give a mother who was worried about her toddler's habit of breath holding?

THINK ABOUT IT

Write down a list of behaviours that are generally disapproved of by people in the society in which you live.

Write down a list of behaviours that are expected or encouraged by people in the society in which you live.

If you are carrying out this exercise in a group you could compare your lists with those of others.

DEFINITION

socialisation   the way that children's behaviour is moulded so that their behaviour conforms to that which is expected in the society in which they live

ANTISOCIAL BEHAVIOUR (SWEARING, LYING AND STEALING)

During childhood, children are expected to learn how to behave in a way that is acceptable in the society in which they live. This process of learning to behave in a socially acceptable way is called **socialisation**.

As a rule, people who live in a particular society or culture have an understanding of how members of that society should behave.

If you compared your lists with others, you probably found that, although your lists were varied in the items you wrote down, there was general agreement. Some behaviours that meet with society's disapproval are so important that there are laws passed to discourage them. For instance, murder and stealing are all against the law. Some behaviours are not against the law but are still not socially acceptable, such as picking your nose in public or eating peas off your knife. These behaviours are generally behaviours that are considered bad manners. In the same way there are some things that we must do by law, such as paying our taxes. Some behaviours are encouraged because they are good manners, such as saying 'Please' and 'Thank you'.

Parents, carers and childcare practitioners become concerned if children are slow to learn socially acceptable behaviour, since there are serious consequences if children reach adulthood displaying behaviour that meets with disapproval or even leads to them coming into contact with the law. There will always be some children who fail to learn socially acceptable behaviour either because of their individual makeup or negative influences in their upbringing. Many children exhibit an aspect of antisocial behaviour at some point in their childhood, which may worry their parents and carers but, if handled sensibly, need not have long-term consequences.

Swearing

Every language contains words, generally with a sexual or anal meaning, that are considered inappropriate for 'polite' company. Swear words are powerful words and, although most of us occasionally use them in times of stress, we would not like children to grow up using 'bad language' regularly.

- Children learn by copying others and are more likely to copy the people who are most important to them. For young children this will be their mothers and fathers and childcare practitioners. As children grow older they will be influenced more by their friends.

- Children will repeat something that is rewarded. Getting attention for swearing, even if this is negative attention, will encourage the behaviour to continue.

- Children learn by experimenting and using words playfully, they will experiment using swear words in the same way.

Four- and five-year-old children often go through a stage of experimenting with swear words. Adults use these words with emphasis and children pick them up very easily. They will try out the word for themselves and will be excited if adults react with horror or upset. They will have found a very efficient way of gaining attention and will tend to repeat the word to see the effect it has on other occasions. Boys seem to swear more than girls, especially between the ages of 5 and 6 years. It coincides with a time when they are experimenting with 'manly' behaviour.

How to deal with swearing

- Ignore the behaviour.
- Enlist the help of all the adults who care for the child.
- At another time, let the child know that the word is not a nice one.
- Give the child a more appropriate word to use.
- If the swearing persists, discuss your concerns with the child and the child's parents.

- Tell the child that you want to help him learn how to control the swearing and agree with him an appropriate form of discipline. You might suggest that if he swears at nursery he might not be allowed to use the computer for the rest of the session.

- Congratulate the child for being able to control himself when he is successful.

Lying

All children say things that are not true at some point in their childhood. Young children may not fully understand what they are saying is not true, or that it is important to tell the truth. However, adults often get very upset if they discover a child's untruth, and may wonder how they can raise the child to become an honest, responsible adult.

Why children say things that are untrue

Small children of around 4 and 5 years frequently say things that are not true.

- They have very active imaginations and have a rich fantasy world. Adults often join in with their fantasies. A child may tell you that they have seen a tiger in the garden and the adult may comment that this is exciting and ask what the tiger was doing. This sort of untruth is only a difficulty if the child retreats so far into her fantasy life that she fails to develop appropriate friendships with children of her own age. Children, when gently questioned, are able to tell the difference between fantasy and reality.

- Sometimes, children will tell you something that is untrue, but which they wish to be the case. For instance if an older brother has been on a school trip to the seaside, the child might tell you that she has been on the trip too. If you know the child is lying, the most appropriate way of dealing with the situation is to say something like, 'Your brother had a lovely day didn't he, I can understand why you want to go to the seaside as well'. This way you are encouraging the child to tell the difference between what is reality and what they want to have happened.

- Children observe adults telling 'white lies' and will copy this sort of behaviour.

- A child might accidentally break something and be very frightened of the adult's response when the misdeed is found out. When asked who broke the object she may say that it was someone else. The angrier the adult is, the more the child begins to believe her story, because she really wishes it were true. In these situations, adults need to understand that the accident was just that, an accident and should try not to be too angry. You need to encourage the child to take responsibility for what she has done and this will not happen if the child is frightened. For instance if you discover that a book has been scribbled in you could say, 'Oh, dear, there is scribble in this book, I wonder how it got there?' This is much more likely to encourage the child to tell the truth. When she admits that she did it you could praise her for being truthful but also explain that scribbling in books is not a good idea because it spoils them and that you do not want her to do it again.

Stealing

Young children have to learn about what belongs to them and what does not. Children of 4 years and below will automatically assume something is theirs unless they are told it is not. Learning about possession is not easy. Consider the following scenario. A three-year-old is taken to a post office/shop with his mother. He picks up a leaflet from the counter and his mother makes no response. He explores it happily and puts it in his pocket. Later he picks up a birthday card and puts it in his pocket along with the leaflet. His mother is very cross and tells him that he must put the card back because it is wrong to steal. This must be very confusing. If adults react too strongly to an incident of 'stealing' there is the danger that the child will start covering up his actions and the behaviour will become more entrenched. Instead, it is wise to gently guide the child into an awareness of what is theirs and what belongs to others.

Helping children understand about possession

- Establish simple rules such as, 'Do not take anything from a shop without asking first' and 'Do not leave anyone's house with anything without asking first'. When playing with other children you could have a rule such as, 'Do not take a toy from a child without asking first'.
- Explain the concept of borrowing and returning toys.

How to help children who have taken something that is not theirs.

- Do not lose your temper. Use the incident as an opportunity to reinforce teaching about possession. Explain that what she has taken does not belong to her.
- Talk to the child, try to understand why the incident happened and help the child understand why she took the object.
- Encourage the child to decide how she is going to handle the situation, for instance giving the object back and saying sorry.
- If the child continues with such behaviour, discuss with the child what she considers to be a suitable punishment, perhaps a short period of 'time out' is appropriate.
- Persistent taking of objects may be a sign of emotional distress. Sometimes children, who feel at an unconscious level that their needs are not being met, may collect items and hide them as a substitute. In many cases, the child feels a lack of love or attention. Professional advice and support should always be sought in these cases.

GOOD PRACTICE

Persistent stealing may be a sign that a child is in emotional distress. If childcare practitioners are concerned, they must discuss the issue with the child's parents and suggest that the parents take professional advice from their GP or health visitor.

✔ PROGRESS CHECK

1 At what age is it common for children to swear?
2 What should a childcare practitioner do if she hears a three-year-old child swear?
3 A four-year-old child tells you that she has a pet pony and you know that this is not true. What should your reaction be?
4 A two-year-old child has 'stolen' a bag of crisps from someone else's lunch bag, her father hears about it and wants to punish the child. As the child's key worker, what do you say to the father?

FURTHER READING

These books all give useful information about managing children's behaviour.

Berry Brazelton, T. (1992) *Your Child's Emotional and Behavioural Development: The Essential Family Reference Book*, Penguin Books

Douglas, J. (1989) *Behaviour Problems in Young Children*, Routledge

Hilton, T. and Messenger, M. (1993) *The Great Ormond Street Book of Baby and Childcare: From Birth to Five*, Bodley Head

Leach, P. (1988) *Baby and Child: From Birth to Age Five*, Penguin Books

The Health Education Authority, *From Birth to Five*, The Health Education Authority

Woolfson, R. (1998) *From Birth to Starting School: Child Development for Nursery Nurses*, Caring Books

There are many web sites that give good advice about children's behaviour. The number of such sites is increasing all the time and care needs to be taken because some advice may be misleading. It is worth exploring to see what you find. Searching using the word 'Parenting' is particularly successful.

The following are two useful sites.

KidsHealth.org

http://www.cyh.sa.gov.au

More worrying behaviours

PREVIEW

This chapter includes:
- The shy/withdrawn child
- The stressed child
- Anxiety and fears
- The obsessive child
- The depressed child.

In Chapter 6, you learned that most children, at some time or another, will behave in ways that worry their parents and carers. In this chapter, we will be looking at behaviours that are less common although most childcare practitioners will have had experience of helping children with such conditions at some point in their professional lives.

In the previous section, we mentioned that children vary in the way in which they cope with stress. Those of you who have been working with the same group of children for a while often know the personalities of the children so well that you can predict how each child will react in certain situations. Some children will face a new experience with excitement, interacting and exploring straight away. Other children may hold back and quietly size up the new situation before joining in. Some children may retreat and find the whole experience frightening. They may cry and show other signs of being stressed. The children react to the new situation according to their **personality**.

A person's personality is relatively stable so that there are similarities in the way a child will interact with their environment when he or she is 5 years old and they way they will react as an adult.

Of course, the way we behave does change because of the effect of experience and maturity. It is normal for infants to be wary of strangers and become more confident as they get older. Many of us are more self-confident as adults than we were as adolescents. But, despite these developmental changes, most of us recognise that we do have characteristic ways of behaving that continue as we grow older.

The aspect of personality that describes how children interact with their environment is commonly known as the child's **temperament**.

Influences on a child's temperament

27890

There is much debate as to how a child's temperament is formed. Some theorists would say that the child's temperament is inherited and there is evidence that identical twins have more similar temperaments than non-identical twins. Other theorists think that the child's temperament is a result of learning. They would say that children who are rewarded positively for being friendly and outgoing are more likely to adopt this as an aspect of their temperament, whereas children whose explorations are met with a negative response may become shy and withdrawn. Very probably both theoretical approaches have something to offer to our understanding. Children have an inbuilt temperament that they are born with, but this is modified by the way that they are raised and the experiences that they have as they grow up. In addition, there will be an interaction between the child's temperament and they way they are treated and cared for. For example a restless, irritable baby who is difficult to soothe may provoke negative reactions from the mother, resulting in poor mother/child attachments (especially if the mother has little social support).

THE SHY/WITHDRAWN CHILD

Most childcare practitioners will be familiar with children who are shy. These children often find adjusting to nursery life very stressful and are more likely to be found working on their own or alongside an adult, than with a group of children. The child may have a mother who also finds it difficult making friends and finds social situations a challenge.

Characteristics of a shy/withdrawn child.

- The child may lack self-confidence.
- Shy children often speak in a soft voice and can be difficult to hear, often responding non-verbally.
- They seem to be afraid of people and have few friends.
- They are introverted, preferring their own company and working/playing alone.
- Shy children may retreat when being approached.
- They may be afraid to attempt new tasks.

environment

This three-year-old boy is shy about having his photograph taken

Effects

As we noted earlier, there is an interaction between a child's temperament and the people around them. Unfortunately other children and adults sometimes react negatively towards shy children and this can cause problems for them once they start nursery.

CASE STUDY

Lucy is 4 years old. She has only just started nursery because her mother preferred to keep her at home, until she thought Lucy was old enough to cope with all the other children. The childcare practitioner, Pearl, is already worried about Lucy because she plays on her own and often just watches the other children from the side lines. Indeed, she is so quiet that Pearl often forgets that she is there and this makes her feel very guilty. Lucy speaks very quietly and Pearl has noticed other nursery workers getting very impatient with the child. The other children and some of the adults are showing that they are irritated by Lucy when she refuses to join in group activities or refuses to try new experiences. One of the nursery workers confides in Pearl that she resents all the one-to-one attention that Lucy is getting because it is taking the adults away from the other children. The other children are beginning to pick on Lucy and the staff are getting frustrated. Lucy's mother looks unhappy but has not said anything to the staff, leaving the nursery as quickly as she can after dropping off Lucy or picking her up.

1 How is Lucy's shyness going to effect her progress in the nursery?
2 How might the behaviour of some of the adults in the nursery be contributing to Lucy's withdrawn behaviour?

Lucy will be at a disadvantage in the nursery because she is reluctant to try new activities. Indeed, if she is so quiet that the staff sometimes forget that she is there, she may miss out on some activities altogether. In addition, much of the learning in nursery is from working and playing alongside other children. Sometimes shy children will become proficient in 'academic' subjects but fail to develop appropriate social skills. Obviously childcare professionals must be vigilant so that they do not react negatively towards Lucy. They also need to be aware that Lucy's mother may be in distress about the situation but could be too shy herself to discuss it with them.

How to help a shy child

- A key worker system is important. The shy child will find it easier to interact with just one or two adults. The key worker system is discussed in Chapter 2.

- Shy children are often stressed children and so the advice for helping children who are under stress, in this chapter, should be followed.

- The key worker should make every effort to build up a positive, non-threatening, non-judgmental relationship with the child's parents/carers. Shy children sometimes have shy mothers who may find talking to the adults in the nursery very difficult.

- Be observant and do not tolerate any teasing or bulling. This topic is looked at in Chapter 4.

- Look at your own feelings and accept that people who are different from others aren't necessarily inferior.

- You may need to adjust your behaviour to accept the shy child. Do not jump to the conclusion that because a shy child is silent they are uninvolved or unconcerned. The child's silence could mean that she is embarrassed, lacks confidence or fears rejection. The child's silence could also mean that she is thinking seriously and is positive behaviour.

Create opportunities for the shy child to perform tasks that benefit the whole class

GOOD PRACTICE

Do not assume there is something wrong with a shy/withdrawn child. Do not raise your voice and demand that a shy child participates in activities. Do not show that you are anxious or impatient with the child.

- Be friendly and show by your behaviour that you like the child. Gently urge the child to participate, but do not force her. A shy child will often join in a new activity if an adult that she trusts works alongside her, especially if the activity involves other children.

- Speak slowly and softly to the child so that she is not scared. Do not hurry explanations. Adults who are insensitive, loud and boisterous will cause the child to withdraw even further.

- Shy children thrive on praise, as do other children. Be positive about achievements but remember they may be embarrassed if they are singled out for praise in front of everyone else.

- Create opportunities for the shy child to perform tasks that benefit the whole class, such as helping cut up the fruit for snack time.

- Do not try to change the child's temperament. The child has a right to be shy. Many shy children do well academically and the childcare professional should ensure that the child is encouraged to use their ability to concentrate and think reflectively.

✔ PROGRESS CHECK

1 What is the difference between personality and temperament?
2 How would you recognise a shy child?
3 What negative effects do shy children sometimes have on others?
4 Outline how you would help a shy/withdrawn child in the nursery.

DEFINITION

stress   an individual feels stress as a result of an event or events that threaten their emotional or physical safety

DEFINITION

stressor   that which causes the individual to be stressed, such as starting a new school

THE STRESSED CHILD

Children can suffer from **stress** in much the same way that adults do. Many children suffer minor, short-term stress that, with sensitive care, they can learn to cope with. Other children suffer more severe stress and may need skilled, professional help.

You probably were able to produce a very long list for the 'Try This!' exercise. Some **stressors** may be to do with our individual personalities. If you are a perfectionist, you may get stressed if you do not get the highest grade for every essay. Some stressors are external, we may get stressed by too heavy a work load, or noisy neighbours.

Stress affects all of use. A moderate degree of stress is healthy because it makes us alert. Too much stress will make us ill and too little stress will make us dull and depressed. Every individual has a different amount of stress that is right for them. Some people thrive on levels of stress that would make most of us unwell, while others function best in very low-stress environments.

Children suffer from stress in a similar way to adults. Young children may feel stressed about starting nursery, or the birth of a baby brother or sister.

Older children may feel stress because of demands placed upon them at school and relationships with their **peers**. In addition, children may suffer stress because of social changes such as divorce, or on hearing parents discuss money or work troubles in front of them.

Just as adults feel comfortable with different levels of stress, children, too, will all have different reactions and **responses** to stress. Childcare practitioners need to be aware of this and avoid making assumptions about the children in their care. One must not assume that a child who is being brought up in very difficult circumstances is necessarily stressed. It is also misleading to assume that a child from a family where there appears to be no causes of stress, cannot be suffering. The child's temperament may mean that they are stressed in an environment that would not affect other children.

Signs of stress in children

It is almost impossible to give a complete list of signs of stress in children because there is great individual variation. It is also difficult to know the degree of stress. A child may be clingy because of a short-term event such as being left by mother for two hours, or the clingyness may be the result of a long-term stressor such as physical abuse. (Chapter 4 looks at child protection.) To help them understand the children's behaviour, childcare practitioners can draw on information:

- about children and their backgrounds given by the parents
- from previous childcare practitioners
- from professionals involved with the child and the family, such as a social worker
- from child observation
- from what the child says.

The following are some of the signs of stress that you may see in children:

- physical symptoms such as feelings of nausea, vomiting or abnormal appetite; regression in bowel and bladder control; muscular tensions that cause children to be clumsy or to find fine muscle control a challenge
- changes in mood – children may appear apathetic or depressed or they may react in the opposite direction and become hyperactive
- changes in behaviour – children may be clingy, disruptive or throw tantrums; they may comfort themselves by thumb sucking, rocking or masturbation to a degree that is out of the ordinary.

Before you can reduce a child's stress levels, you should try to find out what is causing the stress in the first place and try to modify it. If you are a childcare practitioner, you need to discuss your worries with the parent. Of course, some stressors will be impossible to modify so you will need to think of ways of helping the child deal with the stress herself.

Sometimes excessive thumb sucking is a sign of stress

How to help children cope with stress

- Try to ensure that children are in the best possible physical health. Since children's appetites may be affected, it is especially important to ensure they eat a good, nutritious balanced diet. Adequate rest is essential as is plenty of fresh air and exercise.

- In nurseries, the key worker system, discussed in Chapter 2, will give children a sense of security. The child's key worker will be in a good position to recognise when a child is stressed, support the child and liaise with the child's parents so that the child receives the best possible support.

- A secure, predictable routine, both at home and nursery/school is essential. Such a routine will help children feel in control and will have a calming effect. For some children who come from chaotic households, the calming effect of a predictable framework to the day in nursery will supply a feeling of safety. The more stressed the child, the more important it will be to give plenty of warning if there is to be any change to the daily routine and children will need extra warning when it is time to change from one activity to another. Troubled children benefit from being told that in five minutes it will be clearing away time and some nurseries use a dimmer switch for the lights or a giant egg timer to help the children cope with changeover. Within the framework of the day, children should be given the freedom to choose activities for themselves and to explore the resources available. For very stressed children, the childcare practitioner will have to supply more structured activities, as too much choice will be difficult for these children to handle. Working alongside an adult in a cooking activity, or a creative activity with clay will give children a feeling of safety and containment.

- Give stressed children plenty of one-to-one attention. They need the opportunity to discuss their feelings, but you should never probe or force a child to talk. Imaginative and small world play are useful ways for

'It's tidy up time in five minutes'

children to express emotions that cannot be verbalised, either because the child does not have the language skills, or would rather not express their feelings in words. Let children know that everyone feels stress at some time and that it is all right to feel angry, scared or lonely. Let children know that others have the same feelings in similar situations. There are many good books available that can be used with small children to help them understand the particular situation in which they find themselves. There are books that deal with divorce, bereavement, and changing schools.

- Children under stress very often have low self-esteem, they may feel inadequate and worthless. Chapter 3 looks at ways that childcare practitioners can help children with low self-esteem.

- Be positive, praise children for behaving in ways that you approve of, and let them know that you have noticed when they are trying hard, concentrating and so on.

- Sometimes stressed children regress and may ask to be put back into nappies, or be fed when they were feeding themselves independently before. Children who ask for help should be given it, but let them know that you recognise that this is a temporary state of affairs and that tomorrow they may feel like feeding themselves.

- Very stressed children may find it difficult forming appropriate relationships with other children. Childcare practitioners should monitor this aspect of development and supply activities that encourage children to work and play alongside others.

✔ PROGRESS CHECK

1 **Why is it incorrect to assume that children will react in the same way to a particular stressor?**

2 What are the signs of stress in children?

3 What are the benefits of a routine for children who are stressed?

4 What sorts of activities are particularly helpful for stressed children?

ANXIETY AND FEARS

In the previous section, we have looked at the children who are under stress. In this section, we will be looking in more detail at children who are stressed because they are anxious, or have fears.

The most usual response to stress is **anxiety**. For adults, common causes of anxiety are new situations, meeting new people, being asked to speak in public and taking exams. We may feel worried and apprehensive and a little bit fearful. We may experience physical symptoms as well such as butterflies in the stomach and a dry mouth.

Although anxiety is uncomfortable it has an important role to play.

- Being anxious puts us in a state of alert. We are better able to respond to threatening or dangerous situations. Being anxious about heights may prevent us from hurting ourselves by being over-adventurous.

- People perform better with a moderate degree of anxiety, although too much anxiety hinders performance. Some students need to feel a little bit anxious about an approaching deadline for an assignment before they start to work.

- Children need the experience of dealing with anxieties so that they are prepared to handle challenging and unsettling experiences as they grow older.

Common anxieties and fears in children

THINK ABOUT IT

We all feel anxious at some time or other. What situations make you feel anxious?

Can you describe what being anxious feels like?

Do you think anxiety is always a negative experience, or can you think of situations when anxiety is helpful?

- Some reactions are instinctive. If a new baby feels that he is about to be dropped, he will produce a violent response where his arms shoot out sideways and come together as if to grab on to something or someone. At the same time, the baby will give a startled cry to attract attention.

- Babies show fear or wariness of strangers and will cling on to their parents if they see people they do not recognise.

- As children's imaginations develop, between the ages of 2 and 6 years, children begin to have fears about things that are not real such as monsters and ghosts. This can generalise to a fear of the dark.

- At this age, children are learning about their own aggressive feelings and are afraid of aggression in others.

- Other common fears between the ages of 2 and 6 include fear of loud noises, blood, insects, being left alone, animals and heights.

- Older children have fears that reflect real circumstances, such as a **fear** of being hurt, natural disaster, a parent's death and fear of failure.

- Fears tend to be more common at times of rapid learning and increasing independence.

DEFINITION

fear fear is an acute form of anxiety, when an individual wants to avoid the threat at all costs. Examples of fears for adults would be a fear of the dentist, or a fear of heights

Helping a child who is anxious or fearful

Although it is not possible for parents and childcare professionals to totally eradicate children's fears, it is possible to help children take the fears less seriously and to learn from them. This is not always easy because sometimes the children's fears remind the adults of fears that they had in the past and may be still unresolved. It helps to remember that fears are normal and that learning to handle fears is an important part of growing up.

Has the child got a problem?

If the child's fear is common for his age and if he is responding to this fear as any child of his age would, then it is unlikely that there is a cause for concern. Parents and childcare professionals should offer reassurance and practical help such as providing a night light if the child is afraid of the dark.

If the fear is unreasonable and out of all proportion to the situation, the child may need professional help, especially if the child's development in other areas seems affected.

GOOD PRACTICE

- In helping children who have fears and anxieties, look back at the suggestions for helping a child who is stressed.
- Take the child seriously. The fear may seem trivial to you but is very real for the child.
- Talk to the child about his fear. Often, talking will put things into perspective. Talking will often take the power out of emotion.
- Reassure the child that as they get older they will learn how to handle the fear, but for now you know it is scary.
- Allow the child to regress, baby him if that is what he wants, but also praise any efforts he makes to be brave.
- Tell him that other children have these fears too. Suggest to older children that they discuss how their friends deal with scary feelings.
- Tell the child about fears you had at his age and how you learned to overcome them.
- If a child overcomes a fear, point this out to him and refer back to it when he has another fear. You might like to say something like, 'Remember when you were afraid of the Hoover? You got over that and soon you won't be afraid of thunder anymore'.
- Do not change your lifestyle because of the child's fears. If a child is afraid of dogs it will make things worse if you cross to the other side of the road if you see one.
- Teach the child to tell you how frightened he feels by using a rating scale. A mild fear can be given a score of 1, whereas a severe fear may need a score of 10. Younger children can be taught to tell you how full up of fear they are. A mild fear might mean they are scared up to their knees, while if they are full up to their heads, they are petrified.
- Teaching the child coping techniques can help. You could teach the child positive statements to say such as, 'I can do this' or 'I will be OK', when he feels anxious. Relaxation techniques and breathing exercises can also be helpful.

More severe problems

Occasionally, children develop severe anxiety disorders and expert help will be needed. It is estimated that between 5 and 20 per cent of all children have an anxiety disorder, making it one of the most common mental health problems that children face. Children who have an anxiety disorder are more likely to suffer from serious depression as adults. The main anxiety disorders seen in children are:

- generalised anxiety disorder (GAD)
- separation anxiety disorder (SAD)
- social phobia.

Generalised anxiety disorder

The diagnosis of GAD is relatively uncommon in children, but it is thought that there may be a degree of under-diagnosis because the children often achieve well at school despite their condition.

Children with GAD have severe and uncontrollable anxiety about everything, even when there is no realistic cause for worry. Common worries are:

- being on time for appointments
- school performance
- changes in routine
- health
- family matters
- the future.

These worries are accompanied by physical symptoms such as headaches, muscle tension, poor concentration, problems with sleeping and irritability.

If the child has shown at least one sign of anxiety for more days than not in the past six months, then a diagnosis of GAD will be made by the child's psychiatrist.

Separation anxiety disorder

Normal children will go through stages when separation is a challenge. Children with SAD show behaviour that is not normal. They show extreme fear of being taken away from their parents. Children old enough to explain their feelings will say that they are afraid that something terrible will happen to them or their parents. They may refuse to sleep alone and may complain of nightmares or physical symptoms such as stomach ache or headaches. In addition, children with SAD may show signs of **agoraphobia**.

A diagnosis of SAD will be made if the child has shown symptoms of excessive anxiety for at least four weeks.

Social phobia

Many children are shy or withdrawn, however some children's shyness is outside the bounds of normality. Children with a social **phobia** are painfully shy. They fear a wide range of situations such as speaking in class, PE lessons, speaking to adults or other children, starting or joining conversations, eating in public and taking tests. Because they fear people that they do not know, these children may find making friends very difficult.

Children who have a social phobia often remain isolated as adults.

Causes of anxiety disorders

Anxiety disorders have been shown to be a result of a combination of environmental and biological influences.

Environmental influences

Anxiety and fear can be learned by watching others who are anxious, or by an experience that causes anxiety. If a child's mother is afraid of dogs and will avoid them at all costs, the child is likely to have a fear of dogs as well. Children who are timid and afraid to take risks sometimes have a parent who behaves in the same way.

DEFINITION

agoraphobia agoraphobia is a fear of having a panic attack in an open or public place where help may be unavailable, or escape impossible

---

DEFINITION

phobia phobias are intense, irrational fears of a situation that most people would not consider particularly dangerous, such as touching feathers

---

Biological influences

Some children are born with a tendency to be shy or tentative in unfamiliar situations. When these children are investigated, it is found that they have high levels of arousal in part of their brains. It is thought that anxiety reactions are caused by an imbalance in brain chemistry. There is evidence that early, stressful events can cause changes within the brain.

Treatment for anxiety disorders

Professional treatment is required for children with anxiety disorders. In order to decide if a child needs treatment, the professional, usually a GP or a child psychiatrist, will want to know how long the child has been anxious and what steps have been taken already to try and help. The child's key worker or teacher will be able to give information about how the child is behaving at nursery or school. The professional will then decide whether the child's symptoms are normal for the child's age, or are, in fact, symptoms of a more serious problem. Parents will be asked to evaluate how much the anxiety stops the child leading a normal life. The professional will also investigate the child's environment to see if there is something that may be making the child's anxiety worse. It may be apparent that one or both of the parents are anxious, or that there has been a recent upheaval in the family.

Treatments can involve medication, cognitive behaviour therapy and being taught to relax. Therapies are discussed in detail in Chapter 5.

✔ PROGRESS CHECK

1 What are the benefits to an individual of being anxious?

2 What are typical fears for a five-year-old child?

3 What are typical fears for an older child?

4 When would you consider asking for professional help for a child ?

5 Outline how you would help a child who had a fear of the dark.

6 What is a generalised anxiety disorder?

7 How are anxiety disorders treated?

DEFINITIONS

obsessive compulsive disorder an anxiety disorder marked by the presence of obsessions and compulsions severe enough to interfere with normal activities

obsessions obsessions are repeated, unwanted thoughts, often connected to fears about being unclean

compulsion compulsions are repeated, purposeless behaviours

THE OBSESSIVE/COMPULSIVE CHILD

In some children, anxiety is shown by the child having obsessive thoughts or showing compulsive behaviour. Some children with very severe symptoms are diagnosed with having an **obsessive compulsive disorder**.

In pre-school children it is normal to see behaviour that resembles **obsessions** and **compulsions**. Bedtime is a common time for these rituals to be acted out, with children refusing to settle for the night unless they have the same soft toys with them, are given the same number of kisses and have a glass of water put in exactly the same place each night. These bedtime rituals can become quite complex and children can become distressed if the ritual is not performed in exactly the same way every night.

The use of ritual by children varies according to their age.

- Aged about 2 years and 6 months, ritualised/compulsive behaviour is common at mealtimes, bathtime and bedtime. It helps provide a sense of security for children.
- Between 5 and 6 years, ritualised behaviour can be seen in the way children play games with rules and rhymes.
- Older children may start collections of objects and may become obsessed with hobbies.

Ritualised behaviour helps the child cope with anxiety and, when shared by other children, helps with social development.

Very occasionally children have such severe obsessions and compulsions that normal life is disrupted and the diagnosis of obsessive compulsive disorder (OCD) is made.

Symptoms of OCD

- There is a presence of obsessions and compulsions that the child cannot control.
- Sometimes the obsessions are not only senseless, but they are unpleasant and distasteful. Some children have repeated thoughts about killing family members. Obsessions can be about dirt and germs or the exact positioning of articles, or the need to do things in the same way or order all the time.
- For children these obsessive thoughts are a way of imposing order on their anxiety.
- Common compulsions include excessive hand washing, linked to obsessions about cleanliness, hoarding objects and seeking reassurance that something has or has not happened.
- Symptoms can vary in their severity. Sometimes the child will be severely affected, while at other times, the symptoms will be less noticeable.

Common compulsions include excessive hand washing

- Symptoms are time consuming. Children who have obsessive thoughts about cleanliness may spend half an hour washing their hands or 20 minutes brushing their teeth.

- Older children may realise that the symptoms are unreasonable and may be distressed by their condition.

- Children with OCD may be successful at school but have difficulty getting work done at home because it has to be perfect.

- Occasionally, obsessive compulsive behaviour can be an indication that the child is being abused. Child protection is discussed in Chapter 4.

Incidence

About 3 per cent of the general population have OCD. In 50 per cent of cases, the condition appears before the age of 15, with some children being diagnosed before they start school. The peak onset is around 10 years of age with twice as many boys being affected as girls. Twenty per cent of children have another family member with OCD and it is thought that it is caused by a disturbance in the brain chemistry.

Treatment

The usual treatment is a mixture of behaviour therapy, cognitive therapy and drug treatment. Therapies are looked at in Chapter 5.

✔ PROGRESS CHECK

1 Explain the difference between obsessions and compulsions.
2 How might you recognise a child with OCD?
3 What is the incidence of OCD in children?
4 How is OCD treated?

THE DEPRESSED CHILD

Most of us get depressed from time to time, sometimes because of a specific event that has depressed us, sometimes for no particular reason at all.

Depression can affect the way we behave. We may sleep more or watch more TV instead of going out and meeting our friends. We may find that our eating patterns change. Some people will eat more, while others will go off their food. Depression may make us feel tired and irritable. We may start to feel that we are worthless, we may have feelings of low self-esteem and feel inadequate.

Depression is a normal response to adverse life events. Common situations that make us feel depressed would be failure at work or college, the death of a loved one or the failure of a relationship. Illness or increasing infirmity can also precipitate depression. Depression is only considered abnormal if the depth of depression is out of all proportion to the event, or

TRY THIS!

Depression affects how we behave, feel and think. Using these words as headings, write down how depression affects you. If you are doing this exercise in a group situation you may like to compare lists.

Sometimes we eat more when we are depressed

depression continues well past the time that others, in similar situations, would have recovered. Some people with a depressive illness feel depressed for no external reason at all.

Children, as well as adults, will feel depressed from time to time as a normal response to things that are happening to them. Some children will be diagnosed as having a depressive illness which prevents them from leading normal lives.

Incidence

It is estimated that five per cent of children and adolescents suffer from a depressive illness. One to two per cent of children from 5 to 11 years old are diagnosed with depression, rising to 8 per cent for adolescents. In childhood, there are equal numbers of boys and girls who are depressed but, in adolescence, more girls than boys are affected.

Diagnosing depression in children

Because most children feel sad or depressed at some time or other it may be difficult for parents and carers to recognise that a child's level of depression is not normal and that the child has a depressive illness. In addition, the symptoms of depression in children are not always the same as for adults. Depressed children are often moody and difficult to please. They may swing between great sadness and sudden anger. Some children do not realise that they are depressed and it takes a parent to realise that all is not right. Professional help should always be sought if parents and carers are worried.

There are two types of depression seen in children:

- major depression, which lasts at least two weeks
- dysthymic disorder, milder than major depression, but which lasts for a year or longer.

Major depression

Children with major depression can appear to be quite cheerful at times, but when they are feeling low, they are very low. They have trouble paying attention and may stay in their room, not taking part in any of their favourite pastimes. Depressed children may feel tired, cry, think about death and worry that they are going mad.

Children are diagnosed as having a major depressive disorder if they have experienced depressive symptoms for two weeks to such an extent that it interferes with their lives. Children also have to have had at least five of the following symptoms:

- depressed or irritable mood
- difficulty in concentrating
- fatigue
- feelings of worthlessness
- sleep problems
- appetite problems
- social withdrawal
- restlessness or slowing down
- decreased interest or pleasure in activities
- thoughts of death.

A depressed child may be tired, have appetite problems and withdraw from social activity

Dysthymic disorder

This is a long-lasting depression that seems to be less a reaction to external events, than part of the child's personality or temperament.

Causes of depression in children

Research has shown that depression runs in families. Children whose parents have depression are 50 per cent more likely to be depressed than children from parents who are not affected. It is thought that children who suffer from depression are born with a chemical imbalance in the brain which leads them to have a susceptibility to depression. If such children are faced with adverse life events they are, therefore, more likely to experience a depression than other children. They are also less able to deal with depression than other children. Even children with no family history of depression can be affected if they suffer extreme negative experiences.

Treatment for depression in children

Early diagnosis and treatment is vital because the longer children keep feelings of sadness, loneliness and helplessness inside them, the more ill they will become. The outlook for children with depression, once they have been diagnosed, is very good as it is relatively easy to treat. Skilled, professional help is needed from a GP or a child psychiatrist. Treatment will usually involve:

- medicines that regulate the chemicals in the brain
- cognitive therapy
- family therapy. Treatments are discussed in more detail in Chapter 5.

CASE STUDY

Tom is 7 years old, he lives with his older brother and mother in an inner city area. His mother has suffered depression on and off for most of her life and recently his father left home. Tom's teacher has become concerned because he has lost motivation with his school work. He spends a lot of time staring out of the window when he should be working. Tom's teacher has asked him what is wrong and he has told her that he feels unhappy because he isn't as clever as his brother and that nothing good ever happens to him.

After school, he has stopped playing with the other children and no longer plays football which he used to enjoy. Now Tom spends most of the time watching TV and eating all the biscuits he can find. He has started going to bed early because he says that he feels tired. Tom's mother is too preoccupied with her own feelings to notice Tom's unhappiness.

1 Make a list of all the things that would make you think that Tom was depressed.
2 What should Tom's teacher do in this situation?
3 How might Tom be helped?

✔ PROGRESS CHECK

1 What is the incidence of depression in children?
2 How might depression in children differ from that in adults?
3 What are the causes of depression in children?

FURTHER READING

Atkinson, R., Atkinson, R.C., Smith, E., Bem, D. and Nolen-Hoeksema, S. (1996) *Hilgard's Introduction to Psychology*, Harcourt Brace
Chapter 15 gives a good explanation of conditions such as anxiety, obsessive compulsive disorder and depression. The possible influences of the environment and biological factors are explained. This text is appropriate for students on Level 4 courses.

Bee, H. (1995) *The Developing Child*, Longman
This book has a good explanation of the development of temperament and personality in children and will be appropriate for students on Level 3 and Level 4 courses.

Douglas, J. (1989) *Behaviour Problems in Young Children*, Routledge
This book gives common sense advice about helping children.

Leach, P. (ed.) (1992) *Young Children Under Stress: Starting Points 13*, VOLCUF London
This is an excellent guide from the series of practical guides for early years workers and should be essential reading for all students and practitioners of childcare. It is easy to read and can be recommended for students studying at Level 2, Level 3 and Level 4.

AboutOurKids.org
This is a useful website for childhood mental health issues.

Kidshealth.org
This is a good site for parents and childcare practitioners to access information on child health issues.

CHAPTER 8

Conditions that affect behaviour

This chapter includes:

- Attention deficit disorders
- Tourette syndrome
- Autism
- Fragile X syndrome
- Dyspraxia (clumsiness).

Most children, at some point in their lives, exhibit behaviour that worries their parents and the childcare practitioners who look after them. Many of these behaviours have been discussed in previous chapters. The reasons why children behave in worrying ways has been discussed. Often, it is possible to see the origins of such behaviour in the way that the children have been brought up, or the stresses that they have experienced. In other cases, the children's personality or temperament seems to affect the way they behave. Sometimes, a child's behaviour can be affected by a medical condition that disturbs the normal functioning of the brain and in this chapter we will be looking at some of these conditions.

DEFINITION

developmental disorder
a developmental disorder is a condition that affects the normal development of children. Children with a developmental disorder will not show the behaviour that is expected of children of their age

ATTENTION DEFICIT DISORDERS

Attention deficit disorders are **developmental disorders** where children characteristically show lack of attention, lack of ability to focus and impulsive behaviour. There is some confusion as to what term to use for the condition and you may come across terms such as attention deficit disorder (ADD) and attention deficit hyperactivity disorder (ADHD or AD/HD) or hyperkinetic disorder. Children with this condition are often extremely difficult to handle both at home and at nursery or school.

Signs and symptoms

There is a wide range of severity, with some children showing only mild symptoms and others being so seriously affected that everyday life is disrupted. Symptoms usually become obvious when the child first attends nursery or pre-school. Some children will not be diagnosed until they enter statutory schooling.

Great care must be taken before making a diagnosis of ADD or ADHD. Many 'normal'children will show one or two of the signs and symptoms at some time or another. Treatment may involve the use of powerful medication and it is essential that children are not misdiagnosed. In order to stop this happening it is recommended that the children meet the following criteria before a diagnosis is made.

To be given a diagnosis of ADD or ADHD children need to have abnormal levels of activity and attention compared to other children of their age, observed by all of the following people:

- their parents and carers at home
- the childcare practitioners at nursery/school
- a medical practitioner professional/clinician.

To be diagnosed as having ADD or ADHD children must have suffered the condition for more than six months and the symptoms must have started before the children were 6 years old. Clinicians will also want to ensure that the children are not suffering from another condition such as a hearing disorder, depression or an anxiety disorder that might mimic the symptoms.

Children with ADHD may find it difficult to stay sitting down when required

Signs include:

- focusing on activities for only a short period of time
- leaving activities unfinished
- being easily distracted
- not paying attention to details
- not following directions.
- continuous physical restlessness
- excessive squirming/fidgeting during activities at home and nursery/school
- difficulty in remaining seated when required
- inability to keep still in situations such as mealtimes and story time
- blurting out answers before hearing the full question
- difficulty in waiting.

Other disorders that may coexist with attention deficit disorders

- Children may show signs of depression.
- Children may have a specific learning disability such as dyslexia. **ADHD** is not classified as a learning disability, but children with the disorder find that, because they cannot concentrate or stay on task very long, they fall behind in their school work.
- Nearly half of all children with an attention deficit disorder also have an **oppositional defiant disorder**.

Incidence of attention deficit disorders

It is difficult be precise about how many children are affected by ADHD because not all children with the condition are correctly diagnosed and some children who have been given the diagnosis may have been diagnosed in error. Generally, it is estimated that between 3 and 5 per cent of children are affected, although a figure of 10 per cent has been suggested. Fewer children in the UK are diagnosed with the condition than in the USA because different criteria are used to make a diagnosis. Boys are affected more than girls with boys being between two to three times more likely to have an attention deficit disorder than girls. There is some debate as to whether ADHD persists into adulthood. Many children with the disorder will develop into normal, well adjusted, adults but there is a suggestion that the symptoms can persist into adulthood with about 3 per cent of the population being affected.

Causes of attention deficit disorders

There are several suggested causes for ADHD.

- Genetic factors: twin studies indicate that if one identical twin has ADHD then there is an 80 per cent chance of the other twin also being affected. In non-identical twins there is a 40 per cent of both twins being affected. It is often possible to identify a parent (usually the father) of a child with ADHD who also suffered from the condition as a child.

● Abnormal foetal development: in children diagnosed with ADHD, certain areas of the brain which are thought to be connected with attention and movement (the frontal lobes and the basal ganglia) have been found to be about 10 per cent smaller than in unaffected children. This may be due to abnormal foetal development, but could also be a result of the condition rather than the cause of it.

● Chemical imbalance in the brain: it is thought that ADHD may be the result of an imbalance in the chemicals that transmit messages from one cell to the other in the brain. ADHD is more common in children born prematurely than in children born at term and some experts consider that there may be a relationship between prematurity and an imbalance in the brain's chemistry.

Treatments

There is a variety of treatments/interventions that have been shown to be helpful for children with ADHD, but it is essential that if you suspect that a child has the condition, expert professional advice is sought. Many children are suspected as having the condition when their behaviour is perfectly normal for their age. Very often a child may present as being hyperactive because they have no routine in their lives and their behaviour is the result of inappropriate parenting. Thorough investigation into all aspects of the child's life should be carried out, with information from parents and childcare professionals being obtained. Treatment will depend on the child, the family circumstances and the type of childcare and education that the child is receiving.

Medication

ADHD is often treated with stimulant drugs such as Ritalin (Methyl-phenidate) or Dexedrine (Dextroamphetamine). In adults, these drugs will result in increased activity and excited behaviour, but in children with ADHD, the drugs have the opposite effect and will often reduce the child's activity levels. They drugs help the child concentrate and enable them to benefit from schooling. Doctors are not sure how the drugs work, but they may affect the chemical transmitters in the brain.

The drugs are relatively short acting and need to be given under medical supervision because of potential side effects. They are not recommended for children younger than 5 years old.

There is controversy surrounding the use of medication for children with ADHD. There is no doubt that for some children who are severely affected, a closely supervised drug regime has been beneficial. Unfortunately there is evidence of doctors prescribing medication before non-medical interventions have been tried.

Diet

Some foods have been found to adversely affect a few children with ADHD. Such foods are those that contain high amounts of sugar, such as sweets, artificial additives such as tartrazine (a food colouring) and caffeine in tea, coffee and cola drinks. Although removing these from the diet has helped some children, it does not help them all. If parents want to modify their children's diet, expert medical advice should be sought first so that the child does not

Foods containing high levels of sugar, tartrazine and caffeine can adversely affect some children with ADHD

suffer from nutritional deficiencies. A healthy, balanced diet, that follows the Government's guidelines, is still the most appropriate diet for children with ADHD.

Positive behaviour management
Children with ADHD respond well to the positive behaviour management outlined in Chapter 4.

Behavioural modification
Children with ADHD will benefit from a well thought through, consistent behaviour modification programme. Such programmes, planned and supervised by an educational or clinical psychologist, can be undertaken at home or school and are described in Chapter 5.

Parent education
Parents of children with ADHD are under considerable pressure and often feel that somehow they are to blame. Specialists recommend parent education and support groups to help family members come to terms with their child's diagnosis and cope with the day-to-day frustrations that caring for such a child brings. Details of support groups can be found at the end of the book. Parent education aims to give parents as much information as possible about their child's condition. It helps them see things from the child's point of view and helps them see that they are not necessarily the cause of their child's condition. Parents are also taught how to use the positive approaches to children's behaviour outlined in Chapter 4.

Tom is 4 years old and lives with his mother, father and older brother David in the suburbs of a large town. Tom's father has a good job and the family live very comfortably. Tom's mother works part time and Tom attends a local nursery every morning. Tom's mother has found looking after him exhausting. He is on the go from the time he gets up in the morning until he goes to bed at night. He needs little sleep and demands constant attention when he is awake. Tom gets over-excited very easily and often rushes around the house in an uncontrolled way. He has a very short concentration span and never settles to any activity for more than a minute or two. His behaviour is unpredictable and his mother has had to make many more adaptations to the house in order to keep him safe than she had to with David. Taking Tom to the shops or other people's houses is very difficult because he wants to touch and explore everything he sees and will have a temper tantrum if he is stopped. Tom's mother rarely goes out except to work because of his behaviour. The nursery staff have spoken to her and said that Tom's behaviour at nursery is disruptive and that they feel that, unless something is done, they will no longer be able to look after Tom. The strain of looking after Tom is affecting the relationship between the parents. Tom's father thinks that his wife is too lenient and has started to slap the child when he misbehaves.

1 What signs are there that Tom has ADHD?
2 How might his behaviour affect his mother, father and brother?
3 What statutory and voluntary help might there be to support this family?
4 You could use this case study to help you research what help is available in your locality.
5 What could the nursery do to help Tom and his family?
6 What treatment might Tom be given?

✔ PROGRESS CHECK

1 What might lead you to suspect that a child had AD/HD?
2 What actions should childcare practitioners take if they suspect that a child in their care had ADHD?
3 What drug treatments are available to help children with ADHD?
4 What might be the side effects of drug treatments?
5 What are the possible causes of ADHD?

TOURETTE SYNDROME

Tourette syndrome, also known as Tourette's syndrome, Tourette disorder or Gilles de la Tourette syndrome, is a condition of the nervous system where children suffer from repetitive, involuntary movements and vocalisations called tics.

Signs and symptoms of Tourette syndrome

A child with **Tourette syndrome** may show the following signs and symptoms.

- Involuntary motor **tics** or repetitive muscle movements, which can be simple, such as eye blinking, and shoulder shrugging, or complex such as hopping, touching objects, striking out, picking scabs and making funny expressions.

- Involuntary vocal tics, which can be simple such as coughing, throat clearing and making single syllable sounds, or complex, such as, repeating phrases such as 'shut up' or 'you know'.

- Sometimes children will repeat obscene, aggressive or other socially unacceptable words and phrases.

- There may be more than one tic present at once.

- Tics may go away when the child is concentrating or listening to music, but are more frequent in times of stress.

- Tics disappear when the child is asleep.

Many children, perhaps one in five, will have a tic at some point in their lives, but they are usually single and rarely last longer than a few weeks at a time. In children with Tourette syndrome, the tics are different because they come and go and are more complex. The symptoms of Tourette syndrome may be mild, moderate or severe depending on their frequency and complexity. Some children will be relatively unaffected, whereas others may have symptoms that make normal life impossible.

Incidence of Tourette syndrome

It is estimated that Tourette syndrome affects one in 2,000 people. However, this number is likely to be an under-estimation because some individuals have tics that do not interfere with their lives and have never been diagnosed with the condition. Tourette syndrome is more common in boys and usually starts between the ages of 2 and 15 years. The most common age of onset is 7 years. Although children with the condition can improve when they are older, the condition may continue into adulthood.

Causes of Tourette syndrome

Tourette syndrome is an inherited condition. A child with the condition is likely to have someone else in the family with Tourette syndrome. Although the exact mechanism is unknown, it is thought that the condition is due to a chemical imbalance within the brain which leads to a problem with the way different parts of the brain communicate.

In addition to genetic influences, environmental influences on the developing foetus, such as exposure to drugs and other toxins, have been implicated. Babies who have experienced difficulties at or around birth have also been found to be at higher risk of developing Tourette syndrome.

DEFINITIONS

Tourette syndrome an inherited condition in which children show involuntary tics

syndrome a condition where a number of symptoms are found together

tics involuntary movements or vocalisations that are repeated over and over again

---

TRY THIS!

Ask a group of friends or colleagues if they ever had a tic as a child, or have they ever met a child with a tic. Discuss what negative reactions were encountered and how a child with a tic may feel.

Treatment for children with Tourette syndrome

Some children with Tourette syndrome do not need treatment because the tics are not dangerous or harmful. In this case, monitoring and reassurance is all that is required.

If the child is embarrassed, or if the tics are so extreme that normal life is difficult then there are treatments which will help:

● behaviour modification techniques, which are discussed in Chapter 5.

Children can be rewarded for successfully controlling their tics

● relaxation therapy teaches children to relax and stay calm by doing deep breathing exercises and relaxing different muscle groups
● medication such as Haloperidol has been used successfully
● counselling for the child and family has been found to be beneficial.

GOOD PRACTICE

Children with Tourette syndrome may be teased and bullied. Explain to the other children that the child cannot prevent the tics. If teasing or bullying persists, follow the guidelines laid down in the establishment's anti-bullying policy. Children with the condition may find that joining a support group, where they can meet other children with Tourette syndrome, is helpful.

✔ **PROGRESS CHECK**

1 What are the signs and symptoms of Tourette syndrome?
2 What is the incidence of the condition?
3 What treatments are available?

AUTISM

Autism is a developmental disorder that affects an individual's communication skills. It is a life-long disability affecting the way people relate to the

DEFINITIONS

autistic spectrum disorder (ASD) a lifelong developmental disability that affects peoples ability to communicate, use language and make sense of the world. At one end of the spectrum are people who will never live independent lives. At the other end of the spectrum are people who can live independently but who still find relating to others difficult

Asperger syndrome a condition included in the autistic spectrum where individuals are of normal intelligence and can live independently, but have difficulties in relating to others and making sense of the world

THINK ABOUT IT

What ways do we use to communicate with each other?

DEFINITION

triad of impairments the three areas of development, communication, social interaction and imagination, that are affected by autistic spectrum disorder

world around them. Autism can vary in severity and can occur in a variety of forms. At one extreme are people who have very little communication and a learning disability who have to be cared for by others for the whole of their lives. At the other extreme of the condition there are people, with **Asperger syndrome**, who are often of normal or above normal intelligence. These people can function in society, but have difficulty in relating to others. Often, it is not until an individual with Asperger syndrome gets married that the full impact of their inability to make effective relationships is recognised. Such individuals may be diagnosed when they seek marriage guidance. The term **autistic spectrum disorder (ASD)** is used to describe the whole range of ability.

Signs and symptoms of autistic spectrum disorder

There are three main areas of development that are affected:

- communication
- social interaction
- imagination.

These are known as the **triad of impairments** and for a child to be diagnosed with autistic spectrum disorder there must be evidence of problems in all three areas.

In addition, there are a number of associated features that are commonly encountered in children with autistic spectrum disorder.

Communication

Children with ASD will have varying degrees of difficulty with communication, especially social communication.

You have probably thought about spoken language and writing. But there are other ways we communicate with each other, for example through tone

A hug and a smile can communicate a great deal

of voice, gesture and body movements. A hug and a smile can communicate a great deal. We also communicate through painting, drawing and dance and music.

Children with ASD may find difficulties in any of these areas.

- Some children will never learn spoken language, whereas others may speak well and have high levels of literacy. Even if children with ASD speak well, they will tend to use language in an unusual way, often sounding formal and pompous.

- Children may also take statements very literally. If a child with ASD heard someone say that they laughed their socks off, the child might assume that the person's socks really had come off.

- Children with ASD will also find it difficult interpreting the tone of someone's voice, or their facial expressions.

- Children with ASD appear to take little pleasure in social interaction.

Social interaction

Children with ASD have difficulty making and sustaining relationships with others. This will include their parents as well as brothers and sisters, other family members and other children at nursery or school.

- As babies, children with ASD may fail to bond with their mother.

- They may appear distant and aloof to others. Although they may accept social contact from others they remain distant and rarely initiate a social interaction.

- Children with ASD find it difficult to interpret social situations correctly. They may not pick up when people are sad about something and may laugh when such behaviour is totally inappropriate.

- Although some children with ASD can be taught 'rules' that govern social behaviour, these 'rules' will be applied in a blanket way, even if not always appropriate. If they have been taught to shake hands with someone they are meeting and say, 'How do you do?', they may do this to everyone they meet.

Imagination

Children with ASD show difficulties in using their imagination and this is reflected in several ways.

- Children with ASD are unlikely to be able to enter into games of 'lets pretend'. They will not be able to pretend they are someone else, such as a mummy or daddy. It is as if they cannot put themselves in other people's shoes. Children with ASD are unlikely to be able to imagine that an object is something else, such as pretending a plastic brick is a mobile phone.

- When children with ASD use toys they may use them for something different from their intended use. They might never attempt to build with blocks, but line them up according to shape or size. If parents or childcare practitioners try to show them other ways of playing with the blocks, the children may become upset. Sometimes children become fixated on a particular toy such as a spinning top.

185

Sometimes children get fixated on a particular toy such as a spinning top

Other characteristics associated with autistic spectrum disorder

Although not part of the triad of impairments the following features may also be seen in children with ASD.

- A need for routine: children with ASD function best in an environment that is structured and has a routine. If the routine is changed in any way, the children become very distressed.

- Repetitive patterns of behaviour: children with ASD are often seen repeating a behaviour over and over again. It may be a repetitive body movement such as the flapping of their arms, or repeatedly switching on and off a light switch.

- Obsessions: children with ASD often have obsessions or interests. In many cases the interest could be a normal hobby that takes over the child's life to an extent that it is no longer normal.

Incidence of ASD

It is very difficult to give accurate figures as to how many people have ASD because the spectrum is so broad. It is possible that not everyone with the condition has been correctly diagnosed and there are no centrally kept statistics about the number of people who have been given a diagnosis of ASD. In Britain, it is estimated that there are about 500,000 people with an ASD of some sort, about 125,000 being children. (A prevalence rate of about 91 per 10,000 of the population). Four times as many boys as girls are affected.

Causes of ASD

There is no single cause for autism, researchers have suggested that a variety of factors is involved, both genetic and environmental.

- Several studies have found that there are abnormalities in the brains of some people with ASD. Brain cells in some areas have been found to be smaller than normal with stunted nerve fibres. This may affect the way that messages are transmitted in the brain. It has been suggested that ASD is the result of abnormal brain development early in foetal development.

- Some studies have found disturbances in brain chemistry in people with ASD.

- Some other conditions can also cause autistic behaviour, such as **fragile X syndrome**, untreated **phenylketonuria** and **congenital rubella**.

- ASD may be the result of complications of childhood illnesses such as whooping cough and measles.

- There is a strong genetic predisposition to ASD. In families that have one child with ASD there is a 5 per cent chance of having a second child with the disorder.

- Recently there have been concerns that the measles, mumps and rubella (MMR) vaccination given to children in infancy can cause ASD. However, this is not proven and, at the time of writing, the advice is that the risk to children of not being vaccinated outweighs any possible risk of the child developing ASD.

Treatments and interventions

ASD is a lifelong disability which has no cure but there is a variety of approaches that have been found to help children. The approach chosen depends on the exact nature and severity of the child's condition and, at the moment, no one treatment/intervention has been universally adopted as the 'best' method to use. Approaches include:

- SPELL
- TEACCH
- LOVASS
- PECS.

Information about these approaches can be found from the National Autistic Society (their address and website is at the end of this chapter).

Music therapy

Music therapy is used for people with a variety of disabilities, but is particularly useful for children with ASD. Music therapy is discussed in Chapter 5.

How parents can help a child with ASD

Raising a child with ASD can be a challenging and exhausting business. It is important that parents are given as much information as possible about their child's condition and receive as much support as possible from both statutory and voluntary agencies.

How to communicate with a child with ASD

- Use short sentences that contain the essential words only.
- Be as factual and precise as possible.

DEFINITIONS

fragile X syndrome an inherited learning disability which involves a defect in the X chromosome. Learning disabilities can vary from mild to severe. There may be a delay or distortion in speech and language development. There may be behavioural difficulties such as over-activity, attention deficits and autistic-like features

phenylketonuria a metabolic disorder, present at birth that can result in brain damage if the child is not given a special diet

congenital rubella a condition which affects babies whose mothers were infected with German measles in early pregnancy. Children with congenital rubella can be born with hearing and visual impairments. They may also have brain damage

---

TRY THIS!

Investigate your local area to see what **statutory** and **voluntary services** are available for parents with children with ASD. Your local library, health centre and education departments are all good places to start your investigation. The Internet will provide information on support groups. The website for the National Autistic Society is given at the end of the chapter.

Communication learned through music therapy improves the child's communication in other areas

- Children with ASD cling to structure and routine. If you know there is to be a change in routine inform the child well beforehand and tell him exactly what will be happening instead.
- Instead of telling a child what they should not do, tell them what they should do. For example, instead of saying, 'Stop teasing the cat', say 'The cat likes to be stroked like this' and demonstrate the correct behaviour.
- Do not use **sarcasm** or **metaphor**. The child will not understand you and might take what you say literally. It is bad practice to use sarcasm with any child.

Behaviour management

- Use your knowledge of the child to prevent scenes. For example, if a child is calmed by a certain toy, make sure you have it with you on outings.
- Arrange the child's environment so that the child is not over-stimulated by too much noise or activity going on around him.
- Teach the child appropriate ways of dealing with anger and frustration, such as encouraging him to use a punch bag in the garden or allowing him to scream into a pillow.
- Always keep your word. Children with ASD cannot cope with unfulfilled expectations.
- If you mean No say 'No'. Children with ASD cannot cope with 'Maybe'.

- As with all children, children with ASD will respond to the positive behaviour management techniques described in Chapter 4.

How childcare practitioners and teachers can help children with ASD

- If you have concerns about a child and suspect that he has ASD, then you must bring these concerns to the parents as soon as possible and encourage them to seek professional advice.
- If the child is already diagnosed, make sure that you know all about the condition and are confident in participating in any treatment programme that the child may be on, if that is required.
- The establishments' special educational needs co-ordinator (SENCO) needs to be informed so that the 1994 Code of Practice for the Identification and Assessment of Children with Special Educational Needs can be implemented.
- The SENCO will ensure that the other adults in the establishment are aware of the situation.
- Tell the other children about autism, at the level they can understand, so that they know that the child cannot help acting differently.
- Children with ASD are often bullied so look out for this and use the establishment's anti-bullying/behaviour policy to deal with such a situation should it arise.
- Observe how the child interacts with the other children. He may need your help in joining group activities. Encourage activities that require the child to work in co-operation with another child, such as using a see-saw in the outside play area.
- Do not assume that the child has understood what you have said to them the first time. Always check his understanding. Be aware that in group situations, children with ASD may find it difficult to understand conversation that isn't directed specifically at them.
- Children with ASD are visual thinkers, so use visual methods such as pictures to help them learn
- Keep noise and distractions to a minimum and structure the day and the week as far as you can. Children with ASD like routines and need to be able to know what is about to happen. If a routine is going to be changed, start preparing the child a long time in advance.
- Ensure that the child is given tasks that are appropriate for his level of development. If a task is too difficult the child will become frustrated. Use praise and positive reinforcement to raise the child's self-esteem. If the child makes a mistake, praise his effort and show him how it should be done.
- Read through the section on how parents can help. Much of this information is also useful for childcare practitioners and teachers.

CASE STUDY

Trevor is a nursery officer in a busy local authority childcare and education centre. One month ago Luke, aged 4 years, started nursery and became one of Trevor's key children. Luke had been given a priority, full-time place because his mother was finding his behaviour increasingly difficult to cope with at home. Previously, Luke had attended a local pre-school group for mornings only. The staff had found Luke a difficult child to care for. Trevor observed Luke closely and noted that he was showing unusual behaviour. Luke was generally to be found in the large construction area where he spent long periods of time sorting the bricks into sizes. He always lined them up in the same way and became very upset if other children wanted to play with them. At times, Luke could be seen dancing in the middle of the room. At first this behaviour did not concern Trevor, but it soon became clear that Luke's dancing was very repetitive and was little more than spinning around on one spot. Luke showed no interest in what was going on around him in the nursery and did not play with other children. Although Luke could speak, his language was delayed and he never looked anyone in the face when he was speaking to them. During the day, it was very difficult to move Luke on from one activity to another. One day, it was unexpectedly warm and Trevor and the other staff decided to take the children to the park and have their mid-morning snack as a picnic. Luke was very distressed at this change in routine.

1 What signs are there that Luke may have ASD?
2 How might Trevor help Luke while he is at nursery?
3 What difficulties might Luke's mother be experiencing at home?

✔ PROGRESS CHECK

1 What are the triad of impairments seen in ASD?
2 Why is it more appropriate to use the term 'ASD' than 'autism'?
3 What advice would you give to parents about communicating with children with ASD?
4 If you suspected that a child in your nursery had ASD what would you do?

FRAGILE X SYNDROME

In the previous section, it was mentioned that children with fragile X syndrome could have autistic-like symptoms.

Fragile X syndrome is an inherited condition, caused by an abnormality of the X chromosome. Because the X chromosome is one of the 'sex' chromosomes, the syndrome is said to be 'sex-linked'. In this case, mothers are carriers of the condition and pass the condition onto their sons.

Daughters are at risk of becoming carriers or, occasionally, can be mildly affected.

Signs and symptoms

- Children may have developmental delay varying from mild difficulties with school subjects, such as maths, to severe learning disabilities.
- They may have poor speech and communication skills.
- There may be gross motor and fine motor delays.
- Children may show certain physical characteristics such as a long face, protruding ears, poor muscle tone, flexible joints and flat feet. Children may be prone to ear infections, have poor eyesight and boys may have larger than normal testicles.
- Children may be overly anxious, have trouble coping with sensory stimuli such as bright lights and loud noises and show autistic-like features such as hand flapping and avoidance of eye contact.
- Children may say or do the same thing over and over again and dislike changes in routine.
- They may have poor concentration and have frequent temper tantrums.
- Some children may show symptoms of ADHD.

Incidence

Approximately one in 1,000 males have the condition, with one in 600 people being carriers of the syndrome.

Treatment

There is no cure for the condition and children will receive therapies and treatment according to the symptoms they show. Children may benefit from the therapies outlined previously for ADHD and ASD. Children may benefit from speech therapy, physiotherapy and intensive learning support.

> **TRY THIS!**
>
> Look back at the previous sections on autistic spectrum disorder (ASD) and attention deficit hyperactivity disorder (ADHD). Draw up a list of ways that childcare practitioners could help children with fragile X syndrome.

DYSPRAXIA

Dyspraxia, or clumsy child syndrome, is a condition in which there is an impairment of the organisation of movement. Associated with this may be problems in language, perception and thought. Dyspraxia is sometimes referred to as perceptual motor dysfunction, minimal brain dysfunction or motor learning difficulty.

Signs and symptoms

In dyspraxia, children cannot carry out voluntary movements in a skilful way. The following is a list of common difficulties that children experience, but not all children will experience all of these difficulties. Some of these difficulties can be overcome in time, but some difficulties will remain into adulthood. Children with dyspraxia may be of average, or above average

This child is having difficulties knowing the correct sequence of actions to clean his teeth

intelligence, but often behave immaturely. They may find it hard to fit into school because they may not behave in a socially accepted way. Children may experience:

- clumsiness
- poor posture
- awkward walking
- difficulties in throwing and catching a ball
- inability to hop, skip or ride a bike
- difficulties in learning sequences of actions such as dressing or cleaning their teeth
- difficulty in telling left from right
- poor sense of direction
- sensitivity to touch, so clothes may feel uncomfortable, and plasters may be very uncomfortable. Children may find having their teeth cleaned or hair brushed intolerable.
- poor short-term memory
- poor body awareness
- reading and writing difficulties
- inability to hold a pen properly
- speech and language difficulties. Children are often slow to learn speech and then may be incoherent
- inability to answer questions, even though they know what to say

- phobias or obsessive behaviour
- impatience.

Incidence of dyspraxia

Dyspraxia is diagnosed in 2 per cent of the population with 70 per cent of those affected being male.

Causes of dyspraxia

In many children, the cause of their dyspraxia is unknown. Some authorities consider the condition to be due to immaturity of the brain, while others suspect that there may be a degree of brain damage. There are some conditions that affect babies at or around birth that suggest that the children's brains may have been affected in some way. These conditions are:

- prematurity
- placental problems
- umbilical cord around the neck at delivery
- **meconium** passed before birth
- failure of the newborn baby to suck properly.

Treatments for dyspraxia

There is no cure for dyspraxia, although many children improve as they get older. If the condition is identified and treated early, there is a greater chance of improvement. The principles behind treatment lie in teaching children the skills that we take for granted. Professionals such as occupational therapists, physiotherapists and speech and language therapists will be involved. Because symptoms vary from child to child, each child will have an individual treatment programme drawn up to address their particular difficulties. Most treatments will involve a lot of drill and repetition to try to make sequences of movement automatic.

If you suspect that a child has dyspraxia, it is important to seek professional advice as soon as possible. Treatment should be started before the age of 3 years to be most effective, especially if there is a difficulty in language development. If you are a childcare practitioner, liaise closely with the child's parents and express any concerns you may have about the child's progress.

How childcare practitioners and teachers can help a child with dyspraxia

- Find out all you can about the condition. The child's parents and professionals involved will give you the specific information you need to help the particular child.
- Childcare practitioners and teachers should understand how to participate in any treatment programme if this is required during nursery or school hours.
- Children with dyspraxia may have special educational needs. Especially in the nursery years, failure to develop appropriate speech will have an

DEFINITION

meconium the first stool a baby passes after birth. If passed before birth it may indicate that the baby is in distress

adverse effect on the child's ability to access all areas of the curriculum, especially language and literacy.

- Ask your head teacher or line manager to inform your establishment's special educational needs co-ordinator and apply the procedures outlined in the 1994 Code of Practice for the Identification and Assessment of Children with Special Educational Needs.

- Children with dyspraxia may be teased or bullied. Explain to the other children, at a level they can understand, why the child is behaving differently. This may prevent bullying or teasing, but be prepared to use the establishment's anti-bullying procedures/behaviour policy if you are aware that the child is being bullied.

- Give children lots of opportunity to practice their physical skills, lots of repetitions will be needed so that movements become automatic. This is especially appropriate for a child who finds learning to write difficult.

- Use imaginative ways to help the child identify left and right such as marking left shoes in one colour and right shoes in another to match bracelets of the same colour on his wrists.

- Use praise and positive reinforcement to encourage the child, as he will have to use twice as much effort to complete physical tasks.

- Observe the child and be ready to suggest quiet activities if the struggle has become too tiring.

- Children with speech difficulties will benefit from lots of one-to-one therapy with frequent repetitions of sounds, sound sequences and movement patterns to help them become automatic.

- Use mealtimes as an opportunity to give the child foods that help co-ordinate mouth and lip muscles. Crunchy foods such as celery and apple encourage chewing. Smearing a child's lips with chocolate will encourage him to lick it off. Blowing bubbles also encourages the co-ordination of mouth muscles.

- Children whose language is severely affected may use a signing system such as Makaton. You will need to become familiar with the signs so that you can communicate with the child.

Blowing bubbles will encourage the co-ordination of mouth muscles

KEY TERMS

You need to know the meaning of the following words and phrases. Go back through the chapter to make sure you understand them:

ADHD
Asperger syndrome
autistic spectrum disorder (ASD)
congenital rubella
developmental disorder
dyspraxia
fragile X syndrome
insomnia
meconium
metaphor
oppositional defiant disorder
phenylketonuria
sarcasm
statutory service
syndrome
tics
Tourette syndrome
triad of impairments
voluntary service

✔ PROGRESS CHECK

1 What is dyspraxia?
2 How would you recognise a child with dyspraxia?
3 What causes dyspraxia?
4 How would you help a child whose dyspraxia made speech difficult.

FURTHER READING

Aarons, M. and Gittens, T. (1999) *The Handbook of Autism: A Guide for Parents and Professionals* (2nd edition), Routledge
For all-round information about ADS, this book is recommended.

Dare, A. and O'Donovan, M. (1997) *Good Practice in Caring for Children with Special Needs*, Stanley Thornes
This is a good general text for all children with disabilities and special educational needs.

DfEE (1994) *Code of Practice on the Identification and Assessment of Special Educational Needs*
This is a free publication and can be obtained from the DfEE. All childcare practitioners should be familiar with the guidelines for the identification and assessment of children with special educational needs. Parents of children with special educational needs will also find this book helpful.

Mukherji, P. and O'Dea, T. (2000) *Understanding Children's Language and Literacy*, Stanley Thornes
This book has a good section on language and communication difficulties in children, including a section on autism and verbal dyspraxia.

Sainsbury, C. (2000) *Martian in the Playground: Understanding the Schoolchild with Asperger's Syndrome*, Lucky Dip Publishing Ltd

Wilensky, A. (2000) *Passing for Normal*, Scrivener
This book has been recommended as being a useful source of information about Tourette syndrome.

The National Autistic Society, 393 City Road, London EC1V 1NG
Tel: 0207833 2299
Email: nas@nas.org.uk
Website: http://www.oneworld.org/autism_uk/
The National Autistic Society has an excellent information service. The website is very comprehensive and should be the starting point for anyone who wants more information about autism and Asperger syndrome.

Glossary

accommodation the modification of schemas to take account of new information that has been assimilated

ADHD a developmental disorder which has three subtypes: attention deficit disorder where children have attention and concentration difficulties; attention deficit hyperactivity disorder where children are hyperactive and find self-control difficult; and a combined subtype where children show signs of poor attention and hyperactivity

adaptation changes in thinking and behaviour as a result of assimilation and accommodation

agoraphobia a fear of having a panic attack in an open or public place where help may be unavailable, or escape impossible

anxiety an unpleasant response to a stressor, characterised by feelings of worry and apprehension, often accompanied by physical symptoms

Asperger syndrome a condition included in the autistic spectrum where individuals are of normal intelligence and can live independently, but have difficulties in relating to others and making sense of the world

assimilation the taking in of information about objects or people in a child's environment

attachment in child development 'attachment' can mean the feelings a parent or carer has for a baby or the feelings a baby has towards a significant adult

autistic spectrum disorder (ASD) a lifelong developmental disability that affects peoples ability to communicate, use language and make sense of the world. At one end of the spectrum are people who will never live inde-pendent lives. At the other end of the spectrum are people who can live independently but who still find relating to others difficult

behaviour modification a way of helping people with problem behaviour based on the theory of operant conditioning

behaviour therapy a way of helping people with problem behaviour based on the theory of classical conditioning

behaviour all the activities of an individual (or animal) that can be observed by another individual (or animal)

behaviourism a theoretical approach where psychology is defined as the study of the behaviour of the individual. Psychology is a science and scientific methods are applied. Only behaviour that can be observed is studied. Behaviourists do not study thoughts, feelings and emotions since they cannot be observed and are difficult to study using scientific methods

bonding the initial rush of affection felt by an adult, usually the mother, towards a newborn baby, in the period immediately after birth

classical conditioning a type of learning where an unconscious, automatic response such as a reflex, is triggered by a new stimulus, after the new stimulus has been paired with the usual stimulus that triggers the response

cognitive behavioural therapy this is a general term for treatments that use behavioural modification techniques together with procedures to change the way individuals think

cognitive those processes involved in thinking, remembering, imagining, concentrating and being creative

compulsion a repeated, purposeless behaviour

congenital rubella a condition which affects babies whose mothers were infected with German measles in early pregnancy. Children with congenital rubella can be born with hearing and visual impairments. They may also have brain damage

constructivist model a way of looking at children's learning which explains how children construct ideas and concepts about the world around them

continuum a continuous measure or scale. At one end of a continuum, individuals have a lot of what is being measured. At the other end of the continuum, individuals have little of what is being measured

counselling a therapy which aims at helping individuals with their personal problems, rather than helping individuals with a mental illness

critical period a period of time during development when a child is especially ready to learn a new skill. After this critical period has passed the child may never acquire the skill if they were prevented from doing so at the critical time

developmental disorder a condition that affects the normal development of children. Children with a developmental disorder will not show the behaviour that is expected of children of their age

ego the part of personality that plans and keeps the individual in touch with reality. The result of a balance between the demands of the id and what is 'allowed' by the super-ego

environment a person's surroundings. In psychology, the term is used to describe influences on children such as the quality of parenting, educational opportunities as well as other cultural and social factors

equilibrium the balance between assimilation and accommodation which leads to the modification of schemas

ethnic awareness the ability to recognise an individual's race or ethnic group

ethnic identity children have achieved ethnic identity when they can label themselves according to the ethnic group to which they belong

ethologist a researcher who studies animal behaviour

extinction the phenomenon seen when a response is no longer produced when the conditioned stimulus is presented

faeces a brown, solid material, which is what is left after the gut has digested food. Commonly known as a bowel motion, faeces is released once or twice a day into the toilet (or nappy)

fear an acute form of anxiety, when an individual wants to avoid the threat at all costs. Examples of fears for adults would be fear of the dentist or fear of heights

fragile X syndrome an inherited learning disability which involves a defect in the X chromosome. Learning disabilities can vary from mild to severe. There may be a delay or distortion in speech and language development. There may be behavioural difficulties such as over-activity, attention deficits and autistic-like features

gender identity children have achieved gender identity when they can label themselves as a girl or a boy

gender stability the understanding that one has the same gender throughout life

genes the basic unit of heredity

habit a behaviour pattern that is repeated over and over again until it becomes automatic

heredity the inheritance of characteristics from parents

homeostasis a mechanism designed to keep body processes in balance. If receptors in the body detect that anything is not at the correct level, for instance water level or body temperature, then there will be a physiological and behavioural response set in motion to bring things back to normal

197

id the most primitive part of personality that demands the instant gratification of an individual's needs and desires

ideal self a description of what we would like to be

identification the process whereby individuals take on the qualities and ideas of others

imprinting early learning in which a newborn forms an attachment with some kind of model, usually the mother

improvisation playing music which is created at the time of playing rather than playing music which has been composed previously

Individual Education Plan (IEP) a plan of action drawn up for a child that sets out targets to be achieved in the following few weeks, together with strategies for meeting targets

inherit receiving something from the parents, for example inherited characteristics such as eye colour

inherited a condition or characteristic that is passed down by birth, through families

innate inborn

instinct an innate predisposition to behave in a particular way

intrinsic reinforcement or reward internal feelings of pride, pleasure and satisfaction that make it likely that the behaviour that provoked the feelings will be repeated

intelligence quotient (IQ) a measure of intelligence which compares a child's mental age with their actual age. It is calculated as the child's mental age divided by his chronological age, multiplied by 100. A child of 10 years with a mental age of 12 is said to have an IQ of 120, the average IQ being 100

key worker system used in childcare and education establishments which provide group care. Babies and young children are allocated to a named key worker who carries out the majority of their care during the day and liaises with the children's parents

masturbation the self-stimulation of the genitals by hand or by rubbing them against an object

maturation patterns of change in development that are sequential and genetically programmed

meconium the first stool a baby passes after birth. If passed before birth it may indicate that the baby is in distress

mental representations thoughts in an individual's mind that take the place of an object or events in the physical world. These thoughts may be simple such as a mental picture of an object, or more complex thoughts used when we are thinking about mathematical problems or philosophical issues

metaphor a figure of speech such as, 'Her words stabbed at his heart'

nature/nurture debate the discussion about the relative importance of heredity (nature) as opposed to upbringing and environment, on an individual's behaviour

normative assessment comparing what an individual child can do, with what other children of the same age can do

normative development the description and identification of what children can do at a particular age, based on observing large numbers of children

object permanence when a baby demonstrates that they understand that an object exists even if they cannot see it, they are said to have achieved the concept of object permanence

objective a judgement based on independent evidence, not influenced by personal feelings or opinions

observational learning learning a behaviour by copying another person

obsessions repeated, unwanted thoughts, often connected to fears about being unclean

obsessive compulsive disorder an anxiety disorder marked by the presence of obsessions and compulsions severe enough to interfere with normal activities

obsessive, compulsive behaviour behaviour seen in people who have an anxiety disorder, when individuals have an irresistible urge to repeat certain behaviours such as washing their hands

operant conditioning a type of learning where the behaviour that is rewarded (reinforced) is likely to be repeated

oppositional defiant disorder a disorder, more common in boys, where children are stubborn, defiant and have outbursts of temper

partial reinforcement where a behaviour is not reinforced on every occasion, but only some of the time

peer group a group of friends or associates of the same age

peers the friends or acquaintances with whom you associate , both within a school/ college setting or workplace, or socially. In childhood, peers are children who associate together and who are roughly the same age

personality a term used to describe a range of characteristics that describe the way in which individuals typically interact with the people and the world around them. A person can be shy or gregarious, confident or uncertain, dependent or independent

phenylketonuria a metabolic disorder, present at birth that can result in brain damage if the child is not given a special diet

philosophy a system of beliefs concerning the basic truths and principles about the universe, life and morality (or the study of such a system). In a childcare and education establishments the establishment's philosophy would include basic principles about the care and education of children

phobia an intense, irrational fear of a situation that most people would not consider particularly dangerous, such as touching feathers

physiological to do with bodily processes, such as respiration, digestion and reproduction

play therapy a method where children's feelings and emotions can be understood by observing them playing. Play is used as a way of helping children express their feelings and come to terms with life events

Prader-Willi syndrome a genetic disorder that causes low muscle tone, short stature, incomplete sexual development, learning difficulties, behavioural difficulties and a chronic feeling of hunger that can lead to excessive eating and obesity

prejudice negative thoughts, feelings and behaviour towards a group of people

Premack principle the use of favoured activities as a reinforcement to encourage less popular activities

primary health care health care delivered at community level that aims not only to treat illness, but prevent illness through programmes of health education, immunisation, screening and surveillance

propaganda publicity intended to change people's attitudes and behaviour, often used in times of war

psychoanalysis the method of treating people with mental disorders based on the theories of Freud and his followers. Psychoanalysis involves helping a client become aware of previously unconscious processes that have affected their behaviour and emotions

psychotherapy the treatment of mental and behavioural disorders by psychological means

punishment something that reduces the likelihood of a behaviour being repeated, either because it is unpleasant, or something pleasant has been removed

racial prejudice prejudice directed towards people of a different ethnic group

reflex an automatic, physical response which is triggered by a specific stimulus

regression regression is said to have occurred when a child, who has previously achieved a skill or level of independence, reverts back to an earlier level of functioning. A child who has been weaned may insist on a bottle, or a child who was settled in nursery may start crying when the parent leaves

reinforcement anything that increases the likelihood that a behaviour will be repeated. This can be something pleasant such as a reward, or the removal of something unpleasant

role model a term used to describe a person whose behaviour is likely to be copied by another

sarcasm a way of speaking that is meant to give a negative message, although the words imply the opposite. An example of sarcasm would be if a child hands you a scruffy piece of work and you say, 'You've obviously taken a lot of care over that' meaning that they have actually taken very little care

scaffolding helping a child learn by making learning tasks more manageable

schemas basic ideas or thoughts about the environment

screening tests carried out on all members of a target population that are designed to find out if individuals have, or are at risk of having, a condition so that appropriate measures can be taken. All babies are screened either at birth, or at 8 months to see if they can hear properly

self-concept the mental picture that individuals have about themselves

self-esteem the evaluations we make about ourselves. Individuals who think positively about themselves are said to have high self-esteem. Individuals who think negatively about themselves are said to have low self-esteem

self-image how we would describe ourselves

sensitive period a period of time when a child is especially ready to learn a new skill. After this time the child may still be able to acquire the skill with appropriate input from adults. Learning a skill outside of the sensitive period usually takes longer

separation protest when a baby cries and protests when separated from their mother or other person with whom they have an attachment

sex-role behaviour the expected behaviour that is the result of one's sex-role concept

sex-role concept the understanding of how males and females generally behave in any particular culture or society

sex-role stereotyping the over-ridged use of the concept of sex-role, so that no account is taken of individual differences

shaping the learning of complex patterns of behaviour by having the behaviour broken down into small steps and each step being reinforced

social constructivist model a way of explaining children's learning which acknowledges the role of friends, family and other aspects of society in children's learning, in addition to the activities of the child

social referencing behaviour shown by babies or toddlers when confronted with a new situation or object. A baby will turn to look at his or her mother's face and read her expression to see if the situation is safe

socialisation the way that children's behaviour is moulded so that their behaviour conforms to that which is expected in the society in which they live

Statement of Special Educational Needs a document setting out the educational needs of a child which includes a plan as to how the local education authority will meet those needs. A statement follows a statutory assessment of the child's needs

statutory assessment a detailed examination of a child to identify his special educational needs and the best way of meeting these needs. The arrangements for statutory assessments are laid down in the 1993 Education Act

statutory service a service that exists because it is a legal requirement, such as the legal requirement that children are provided with education

stress response   the response that an individual makes to being stressed. These include changes to behaviour, thinking, emotions and physical processes

stress   an individual feels stress as a result of an event or events that threaten their emotional or physical safety

stressor   that which causes the individual to be stressed, such as starting a new school

subjective   a judgment influenced by personal opinions and feelings

superego   that part of the personality that tells us what we should and should not do. The superego contains our conscience and moral values which are formed by the influences of our parents and society

surveillance   a system of regular check-ups, which may include screening tests, to ensure that an individual is progressing well. All mothers are given regular check-ups during pregnancy and babies and children are given regular developmental and health checks throughout childhood

syndrome   a condition where a number of symptoms are found together

systematic desensitisation   a treatment for phobias where the fear reaction is replaced by a state of relaxation. In this treatment, the individual is gradually exposed to progressively more fearful situations

temperament   part of an individual's personality that deals with the person's emotional reactivity, or characteristic way of interacting with their environment. Individuals can be highly emotional or emotionally unreactive, they can be active and restless or placid, they can be very responsive or they can avoid social situations

the security of an attachment   how confident a child is of the attachment figure being there when needed and how the attachment figure is used by the child to give them confidence to explore

the strength of an attachment   the intensity with which attachment behaviours are displayed. A strong attachment may be demonstrated by intense separation protest

tics   involuntary movements or vocalisations that are repeated over and over again

Tourette syndrome   an inherited condition in which children show involuntary tics

triad of impairments   the three areas of development, communication, social interaction and imagination, that are affected by autistic spectrum disorder

urine   a pale yellow liquid, made by the kidneys in the body, which consists of water and chemicals that the body does not need. Urine is stored in the bladder until released into the toilet (or nappy)

vicarious reinforcement   a reward obtained by another for behaving in a particular way that makes it more likely that an observer will copy the behaviour

voluntary service   a service that exists because it meets a need but there is no legal requirement for the service to be set up. A local parent support group would be a voluntary service

zone of proximal development   the difference between what a child can learn on their own and what they can learn with the help of an adult or a more competent friend

Resources

For families and children who are bereaved

Compassionate Friends
6 Denmark Street
Bristol BS 1 5DQ
Tel: 01272 292778

Good Grief
Grindstone Manor Mews
Horrabridge
Yelverton
Devon PL20 7QY
Tel: 01822 854358

For families and children involved in divorce or separation

Gingerbread
35 Wellington Street
London EC2A 3 AR
Tel: 020 7613 5060

National Council for One Parent Families
255 Kentish Town Road
London NW5 2LX
Tel: 020 7267 1361

RELATE National Marriage guidance Council
Herbert Grey College
Little Church Street
Rugby
Warwickshire CV21 3AP

For families and children of prisoners

Prisoners' Families and Friends
106 Weston Street
London SE1 3QG
Tel: 020 7278 9815

National Association for Care and Resettlement of Offenders (NACRO)
169 Clapham Road
London SW9 0PU
Tel: 020 7582 6500

For children with ADHD

Hyperactive Children's Support Group
71 Whyke Lane
Chichester
West Sussex PO19 2LD
Tel: 01903 725182
Email: hacsg@hyperactive.force9.net
Web page: homepages/force9.net/hyperactive/

ADD/ADHD Family Support Group UK
Mrs Gill Mead
1a High Street
Dilton Marsh
Westbury
Wiltshire BA13 4DL
Tel: 01373826045

ADD Information Services (UK)
Foster house
Maxwell Road
Borehamwood
Hertfordshire WD6 1HX
Tel: 020 8905 2013
Milton Keynes ADHD website
Web page: i.am/adhd/

For children with autism

The National Autistic society
393 City Road
London EC1V 1NG
Tel: 020 7833 2299
Email: nas@nas.org.uk
Website: http://www.oneworld.org/autism_uk/

For children with dyspraxia

The Dyspraxia Foundation
8 West Alley
Hitchin
Herts SG5 1EG
Tel: 01462 454986

For children with language disorders (including developmental verbal dyspraxia)

AFASIC-Overcoming Speech Impairments
347 Central Markets
Smithfield
London EC1A 9NH
Tel: 020 7236 3632

I CAN
The National Educational Charity for Children with Speech and Language Disorders
Barbican
Citygate
London EC1Y 8 NA

For children who are being bullied

Childline, a confidential free 24-hour phoneline for children in trouble or in danger.
Tel: 0800 111

Children's Legal Centre
Tel: 01206 873820

Advisory Centre for Education
Education advice line Tel: 020 7354 8321

Kidscape
2 Grosvenor Gardens
London SW1W 0DH
Tel: 020 7730 3300
Email contact@kidscape.org.uk

For information on careers

Clinical psychology
Clearing House for Postgraduate Courses in Clinical Psychology
University of Leeds
15 Hyde terrace
Leeds SL9LT
Tel: 0113 233 2737

Counselling
The British Association for Counselling
1 Regent Place
Rugby
Warwickshire CV21 2PJ
Tel: 01788 550 899

Physiotherapy
Chartered Society of Physiotherapy
14 Bedford Row
London WC1R 4ED
Tel: 020 7306 6600

Occupational therapy
College for Occupational Therapists
Educational and Practice Department
106–114 Borough High Street
London SE1 1LB
Tel: 020 7357 6480

Speech and language therapy
Royal College of Speech and Language Therapists
2 White Hart Yard
London SE1 1NX
Tel: 020 7378 1200

Music therapy
Association of Professional Music Therapists
26 Hamlyn Road
Glastonbury
Somerset BA6 8HT
Tel: 01458 834 919

British Society for Music Therapy
69 Avondale
Barnet
Hertfordshire EN4 8NB
Tel: 0181 368 8879

The Nordoff-Robbins Music Therapy Centre
2 Lissenden Gardens
London NW5 1PP
Tel: 020 7267 4496

Art and drama therapy
British Association of Art Therapists
11a Richmond Ave.
Brighton BN2 3RL

British Association of Drama Therapists
The Old Mill
Tolpuddle
Dorchester
Dorset DT2 7EX

Web sites

United Kingdom Central Council for Nursing, Midwifery and Health Visiting
www.ukcc.org.uk

English National Board for Nursing, Midwifery and Health Visiting
www.enb.org.uk

Royal College of Nurses
www.rcn.org.uk

Index

Page references in italics indicate tables.